Experimental & Theoretical Applications of
Thermodynamics to Chemistry

MAXWELL PRESS

Experimental & Theoretical Applications of
Thermodynamics to Chemistry

WALTHER NERNST

Winner of Nobel Prize for Chemistry

Professor and Director of the Institute of Physical
Chemistry in the University of Berlin

MAXWELL PRESS

Chennai　　　　　　Trichy　　　　　　NewDelhi

MAXWELL PRESS

This edition has been published in india by arrangement with Carson Books, UK

ISBN 978-93-90063-89-5   Maxwell Press

MJP 932   © Publishers, 2023

Publisher :   C. Janarthanan

Publisher's Note

The legacy of a country is in its varied cultural heritage, historical literature, developments in the field of economy and science. The top nations in the world are competing in the field of science, economy and literature. This vast legacy has to be conserved and documented so that it can be bestowed to the future generation. The knowledge of this legacy is slowly getting perished in the present generation due to lack of documentation.

Keeping this in mind, the concern with retrospective acquiring of rare books has been accented recently by the burgeoning reprint industry. Maxwell Press is gratified to retrieve the rare collections with a view to bring back those books that were landmarks in their time.

In this effort, a series of rare books would be republished under the banner, "Maxwell Press". The books in the reprint series have been carefully selected for their contemporary usefulness as well as their historical importance within the intellectual. We reconstruct the book with slight enhancements made for better presentation, without affecting the contents of the original edition.

Most of the works selected for republishing covers a huge range of subjects, from history to anthropology. We believe this reprint edition will be a service to the numerous researchers and practitioners active in this fascinating field. We allow readers to experience the wonder of peering into a scholarly work of the highest order and seminal significance.

MAXWELL PRESS

THE SILLIMAN FOUNDATION

In the year 1883 a legacy of eighty thousand dollars was left to the President and Fellows of Yale College in the City of New Haven, to be held in trust, as a gift from her children, in memory of their beloved and honored mother Mrs. Hepsa Ely Silliman.

On this foundation Yale College was requested and directed to establish an annual course of lectures designed to illustrate the presence and providence, the wisdom and goodness of God, as manifested in the natural and moral world.   These were to be designated as the Mrs. Hepsa Ely Silliman Memorial Lectures.   It was the belief of the testator that any orderly presentation of the facts of nature or history contributed to the end of this foundation more effectively than any attempt to emphasize the elements of doctrine or of creed; and he therefore provided that lectures on dogmatic or polemical theology should be excluded from the scope of this foundation, and that the subjects should be selected rather from the domains of natural science and history, giving special prominence to astronomy, chemistry, geology, and anatomy.

It was further directed that each annual course should be made the basis of a volume to form part of a series constituting a memorial to Mrs. Silliman.   The memorial fund came into the possession of the Corporation of Yale University in the year 1902; and the present volume constitutes the fourth of the series of memorial lectures.

PREFACE

In the following Lectures which were delivered at Yale University, October 22d to November 2d, 1906, I have given, after a general theoretical introduction, a résumé of the experimental investigations which I have carried out in recent years, with the aid of my students, on chemical equilibria at high temperatures.

The study of the results thus far obtained in this field makes it appear probable that there prevails here more conformity to general laws than the two laws of thermodynamics would lead us to expect. To explain these regularities I have developed a new theorem which seems to reveal new truths concerning the relation between chemical energy and heat. It can hardly be doubted that this theorem will prove useful in the treatment of questions other than purely chemical, but in the following Lectures I have not entered into this phase of the subject.

As to the theorem itself, I should like to add

the following general remarks. The large mass of experimental data upon which the theorem has been successfully tested will probably remove any doubt as to whether the formulas developed by its aid have disclosed new laws to us. To decide the question whether the theorem represents only an approximate principle or an exact law of nature similar to the first and second laws of thermodynamics will, however, necessitate many further investigations. From a practical point of view this question is of minor importance, as my formulas are sufficiently accurate for many purposes. From a theoretical standpoint it is, however, of the greatest importance, for the reason that a more exact formulation of the theorem may possibly be found.

In the preparation of these lectures, and in the correction of the proofs, I have been assisted by Dr. K. George Falk, for whose willing and efficient services I wish to express my best thanks.

W. N.

CONTENTS

CONTENTS

LECTURE VI

LECTURE VII

LECTURE VIII

LECTURE IX

LECTURE X

THERMODYNAMICS

AND

CHEMISTRY

LECTURE I

THE GENERAL APPLICATION OF THERMO-DYNAMICS TO CHEMISTRY

.THE application of the first law of thermodynamics to chemistry developed thermochemistry, as is well known.

Let us consider, for example, the reaction between hydrogen and oxygen in the formation of water. The equation is

$$2H_2 + O_2 = 2H_2O + 115300,$$

in which 115300 denotes the number of gram calories developed in the production, at constant volume, of two gram molecules or mols of water in the form of vapor at the temperature of 100° C.

If the reaction is allowed to take place at constant pressure, external work will be done, when, as in our example, the volume is changed by the reaction. Such changes in volume can generally be disregarded, except at exceedingly great pressures, when dealing with solids or liquids, but may be considerable in the case of gaseous systems, for which they can be calculated from the gas laws. For every additional mol of gas formed in a reaction this external work would be RT, where R is the gas constant and equal to 1.985 if we take the gram calorie as the unit of energy. Therefore $115300 + 1.985 \times 373$ would be the heat of formation of two gram molecules of water vapor at constant pressure.

In its most general form the equation of a reaction may be written

$$n_1 a_1 + n_2 a_2 + \cdots\cdots + \nu_1 A_1 + \nu_2 A_2 + \cdots\cdots$$
$$= n_1' a_1' + \cdots\cdots + \nu_1' A_1' + \nu_2' A_2' + \cdots\cdots$$

in which the molecules a are those which take part in the solid or liquid state, and the molecules A are in the gaseous state. The external work would be

$$- \Sigma \nu RT = - \Sigma \nu \cdot 1.985 \, T \, \text{gm. cal.}$$

The heat Q of a reaction at constant volume can also be called the *change in the total energy* taking place during the reaction. The fundamental principle of thermochemistry, derived from the first law of thermodynamics, is that Q is independent of the way in which the system is transferred from one state to the other. (Law of Constant Heat Summation.)

Q', the heat developed at constant pressure, can be found by means of the formula

$$Q' = Q + \Sigma \nu R T.$$

The second law of thermodynamics states that for every chemical reaction a quantity A, the maximum amount of work which can be obtained by the reaction in question, also called the *change in free energy*, has a definite value, and that this maximum work will be done if the reaction proceeds in an isothermal and reversible manner. Moreover the value of A is absolutely independent, like Q, of the way in which the system is transferred from the initial to the final state.

The value of $A - Q$, the excess of the maximum work of an isothermal process over the decrease in total energy, denotes the quantity of heat absorbed when the reaction proceeds in an isothermal and reversible manner, and is called the *latent heat of, the reaction.* As the most important application of the second law of thermodynamics we obtain the following expression for the latent heat of a reaction:

$$(1) \qquad A - Q = T \frac{dA}{dT}.$$

This equation contains in a general manner all that the laws of thermodynamics can teach concerning chemical processes. A and Q are both expressed in units of energy—for example, gram calories—and are both independent of the way in which the reaction proceeds under the aforesaid conditions.

We may at the outset emphasize the fact that every future development of thermodynamics will be an addition to the above equation. As a matter of history it may be stated that this equation was included in the first application of thermodynamics to chemistry by Horstmann (1869). Shortly afterward the problem was treated very thoroughly by J. Willard Gibbs in his great work. Later the simplicity and clearness of this formula was pointed out by Helmholtz.

Let us consider here two important applications of the fundamental formula.

1. The physico-chemical processes such as volatilization, melting, transformation of allotropic forms into each other, are to be treated in exactly the same way as the chemical. For example, the well-known formula of Clausius-Clapeyron,

$$(2) \qquad \lambda = T\frac{dp}{dT}\,(v - v'),$$

in which λ indicates the molecular latent heat of vaporization, p the vapor pressure, v the molecular volume of the vapor, and v' that of the liquid, can be considered as a direct application of our fundamental formula. If the vapor pressure is not too great, v' can be disregarded in comparison to v, and the equation of the gas laws,

$$(3) \qquad pv = RT$$

may be applied. We thus obtain

$$(4) \qquad \lambda = RT^2 \frac{d\,lnp}{dT}.$$

The gas laws can also be written

$$(5) \qquad p = CRT,$$

in which C denotes the concentration of the gas or vapor. Substituting this value of p we obtain

$$(6) \qquad \lambda - RT = RT^2 \frac{d\,ln\,C}{dT}.$$

In this equation $\lambda - RT$ corresponds to Q, being the change in the total energy connected with the process of condensation. As measurements show, the heat of vaporization varies in a continuous and gradual manner and can therefore be formulated

$$(7) \qquad \lambda - RT = \lambda_0 + aT + bT^2 + cT^3 + \cdots\cdot$$

It must be carefully noted that this equation while applicable to every substance, liquid or solid, must be restricted to a definite form of the substance in any one case. We are therefore justified in applying this equation to liquid water, but we must suppose the water to be undercooled when we apply the equation to very low temperatures. Also, if a substance can exist in more than one crystallized form, the above formula must be limited to one definite form at a time. There are, therefore, as many equations of the above form, but with different numerical values of the coefficients λ_0, a, b, etc., as there are different condensed forms of the substance.

Integrating, we find as the formula for the concentration of the saturated vapor

$$(8) \qquad ln\,C = -\frac{\lambda_0}{RT} + \frac{a}{R}\,ln\,T + \frac{b}{R}\,T + \frac{c}{2R}\,T^2 \\ + \cdots + i,$$

in which i must for the present be supposed to be characteristic, not only for any one substance, but also for every definite form of that substance.

2. It is interesting to note that our fundamental formula can be used for a very simple classification of all natural processes, as it is by no means limited to chemical processes.

Natural changes have long been grouped into physical and chemical. In the former the composition of matter usually plays an unimportant part, whereas in the latter it is the chief object of consideration. From the point of view of the molecular theory a physical process is one in which the molecules remain intact, a chemical process one in which their composition is altered. This classification has real value, as is shown by the customary separation of physics and chemistry, not only in teaching, but also in methods of research,—a fact that is all the more striking as both sciences deal with the same fundamental problem, that of reducing to the simplest rules the complicated phenomena of the external world. But this separation is not altogether advantageous, and is especially embarrassing in exploring the boundary region where physicists and chemists need to work in concert.

Since thermodynamic laws are applicable to all the phenomena of the external world, a classification based upon these laws suggests itself. The fundamental formula

$$A - Q = T\frac{dA}{dT}$$

involves the following special cases:

(*a*) $A = Q$: the changes in free and total energy are equal at all temperatures. Then the temperature coefficient of A, and therefore that of Q also, is zero, that is, temperature does not influence the phenomenon in question, at least not as regards its thermodynamic properties. Conversely, if the last condition is fulfilled, $A = Q$. This behavior is shown by all systems in which only gravitational, electric, and magnetic forces act. These can be described by means of a function (the potential) which is independent of temperature.

(b) $Q = 0$, and therefore $A = T\dfrac{dA}{dT}$; or $A = a'T$, in which a' is a constant of integration. A is then proportional to the absolute temperature. The expansion of a perfect gas and the mixture of dilute solutions are the instances of this behavior in which the influence of temperature comes out the most clearly. (Gas thermometer.)

(c) $A = 0$, and therefore $Q = -T\dfrac{dA}{dT}$.

This condition can only occur at single points of temperature; but A can be small in comparison with Q over a considerable range of temperature. As then the percentage variation of A will be large, the influence of temperature must be very marked in such cases (evaporation, fusion, dissociation, i. e., all properly "physico-chemical" phenomena).

Case (c) is evidently not so simple, and has not

given rise to such important hypotheses as case (*a*), which introduced forces of attraction into science, and case (*b*), which was decisive in the development of the molecular theory. (Avogadro's rule.)

The case $A = 0$ and $Q = 0$ would not be a process in the thermodynamic sense. Such cases, however, exist and are of importance (the movement of a mass at right angles to the direction of gravity, passage of one optical isomer into the other, etc.); so it appears that though the science of thermodynamics furnishes important points of view for the classification of phenomena, it is too narrow to cover the whole.

This, of course, is due to the fact that the two laws of thermodynamics are insufficient for a general explanation of nature. They take, for example, no account of the course of phenomena in time,—unlike the molecular theory, in which such a limitation has not thus far been shown to exist.

LECTURE II

DERIVATION OF THE EQUATION OF THE REACTION ISOCHORE $Q = RT^2 \cdot \dfrac{d\ln K}{dT}$

In the following discussion, the influence of the temperature upon the heat of reaction is of the greatest importance. The law of the conservation of energy enables us to calculate this influence from the specific heats of the reacting substances.

If we allow the same reaction to occur, once at the temperature T and again at the temperature $T + dT$, the heat of reaction will be different in the two cases; let these heats be Q and $Q + dQ$ respectively. We can now imagine the following cyclic process to be carried out. Let the reaction occur at the temperature T, thereby developing the quantity of heat Q; after which the temperature of the system is raised to $T + dT$, which will require the introduction of $h'dT$ gram calories of heat, where h' denotes the heat capacity of the substances *resulting from the reaction*. Now let the reaction occur *in the opposite sense* at $T + dT$, a process which will absorb the quantity of heat $Q + dQ$; then let the system be cooled to T_9 whereby the quantity of heat $h\,dT$ will be given off, where h denotes the heat capacity of the *reacting substances.* The system has now returned to its original condition.

Now the law of *conservation of energy* requires that the amount of heat absorbed by the system shall be the same as that given out; i. e., that

$$Q + dQ + h'\,dT = Q + h\,dT,$$

and hence

$$(9) \qquad \frac{dQ}{dT} = h - h',$$

that is, the excess of the heat capacity of the reacting substances over the heat capacity of the resulting substances, gives the increase of the heat of reaction per degree of temperature elevation.

The following diagram illustrates the derivation of the above equation in a slightly different way:

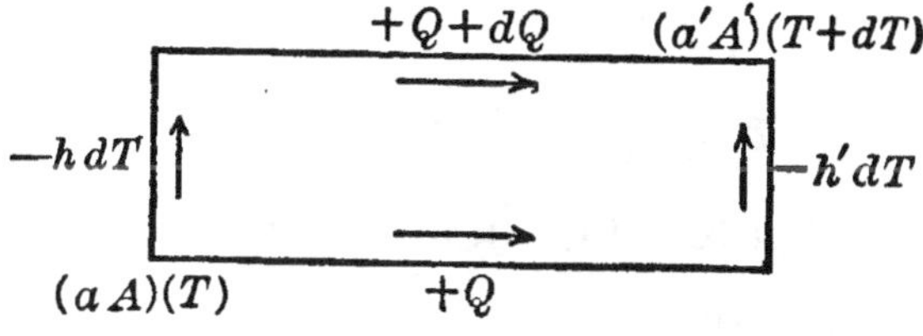

Fig. 1.

From the same initial state, corresponding to the molecules (a, A) and the temperature T_3 we may pass by two different paths to the same final state (a', A') and $T + dT$. Placing the changes in total energy for the two different paths equal to each other, we find

$$Q - h'dT = -hdT + Q + dQ,$$

the above equation.

The great importance of this equation is due to the fact that with its aid, when we know the specific heats, we can calculate the influence of temperature upon the heat of reaction much more accurately than it could be obtained by the direct measurement of the heat of reaction at two different temperatures.

If we apply the heat equation to the process of vaporization, in which

$$Q = \lambda - RT = \lambda_0 + aT + bT^2 + \cdots,$$

we find

$$(10) \quad \frac{d\lambda}{dT} = a + R + 2bT + \cdots = H_v - h_0 + R,$$

in which

$$(11) \qquad H_v = a + 2\beta T + \cdots$$

denotes the molecular heat of the vapor at constant volume, and

$$(12) \qquad h_0 = a_0 + 2\beta_0 T + \cdots$$

denotes the molecular heat of the condensed form of the vapor. We obtain therefore

$$a = a - a_0, \quad b = \beta - \beta_0, \quad \text{etc.},$$

and by substituting in (8)

$$(13) \quad ln\,C = -\frac{\lambda_0}{RT} + \frac{a - a_0}{R}\,ln\,T + \frac{\beta - \beta_0}{R}T + \cdots + i.$$

If we apply the above equation to a chemical process taking place in a homogeneous gaseous phase with coexistent liquid or solid substances, and if we let

$$Q = Q_0 + aT + bT^2 + \cdots.$$

we find

$$(14) \quad \frac{dQ}{dT} = \Sigma\nu H_v + \Sigma nh_0 = a + 2bT + \cdots$$

Furthermore, if we put

$$(15) \quad \begin{aligned} H_v &= a + 2\beta T + \cdots, \\ h_0 &= a_0 + 2\beta_0 T + \cdots, \end{aligned}$$

we obtain

$$(16) \quad \frac{dQ}{dT} = \Sigma\nu a + \Sigma n a_0 \\ \qquad\qquad + 2T(\Sigma\nu\beta + \Sigma n\beta_0) + \cdots,$$

and therefore

$$(16\text{a}) \quad \begin{cases} a = \Sigma\nu a + \Sigma n a_0 \\ b = \Sigma\nu\beta + \Sigma n\beta_0 \\ \text{etc.} \end{cases}$$

We are justified in assuming the above relation to hold true for the specific heat of a substance at different temperatures, from the experimental fact that this specific heat varies continuously and only slightly with the temperature.

We can now proceed to the development of the formulas of chemical equilibria from the fundamental formula

$$A - Q = T\frac{dA}{dT},$$

that is to say, to the derivation of the equation of the reaction isochore. For the end here in view I desire to present this derivation in a somewhat different form from that generally followed.

Let us consider a reaction taking place between solid and liquid substances only, that is, according to our notation previously adopted,

$$n_1 a_1 + n_2 a_2 + \cdots\cdots = n_1' a_1' + \cdots\cdots;$$

or, to use our former example, the formation of two mols of solid or liquid water from two mols of solid or liquid hydrogen and one mol of solid or liquid oxygen.

The question is: How can the formation of water under these circumstances be conceived of as taking place in an isothermal and reversible way? For this purpose two mols of hydrogen and one mol of oxygen are vaporized and brought by means of semipermeable membranes into a space which we may call, as Haber does, the "equilibrium box" and in which H_2, O_2, and H_2O may coexist in the gaseous state in equilibrium. At the same time two mols of the water formed may be supposed to be removed from the equilibrium box through a suitable semipermeable membrane and condensed to solid or liquid water. The concentrations of H_2, O_2, and H_2O in the equilibrium box may be represented respectively by c_1, c_2, and c'.

The work involved in transferring one mol of gas, formed by vaporization under the vapor pressure P, in a space in which the partial pressure of the gas is p, is given by the expression

$$PV + RT \ln\frac{P}{p} - pv,$$

in which V and v represent the volumes of the gas or vapor under the corresponding pressures P and p. But since $PV = pv$, this becomes simply

$$RT \ln\frac{P}{p} = RT \ln\frac{C}{c},$$

in which C and c stand for the concentrations

under the corresponding circumstances. In conveying n mols the work would be, of course,

$$nRT\,ln\frac{C}{c}=RT\,ln\frac{C^n}{c^n}.$$

Now we can easily calculate the maximum work done when hydrogen and oxygen are converted isothermally and reversibly into water, all the substances being in the solid or liquid state. We find

$$A=2RT\,ln\frac{C_1}{c_1}+RT\,ln\frac{C_2}{c_2}-2RT\,ln\frac{C'}{c'},$$

C_1, C_2, C', being respectively the concentrations of the saturated vapor of hydrogen, oxygen, and water. Transformed, the equation becomes

$$(17)\qquad A=RT\,ln\frac{C_1^2 C_2}{C'^2}-RT\,ln\frac{c_1^2 c_2}{c'^2}.$$

The maximum work A must be independent of the nature of the equilibrium box, which only plays the part of an intermediary and suffers no change during the process. This is only possible if at constant temperature the expression

$$RT\,ln\frac{c_1^2 c_2}{c'^2}$$

is constant, and therefore,

$$(18)\qquad\qquad K=\frac{c_1^2 c_2}{c'^2}$$

(K being constant at constant temperature).

This is, however, nothing more than the law of mass action, applied to a homogeneous gaseous system.

If we now apply the fundamental equation

$$A - Q = T\frac{dA}{dT},$$

we obtain

$$RT\,ln\frac{C_1^2\,C_2}{C_1'^2} - RT\,lnK - Q$$

$$= RT\,ln\frac{C_1^2\,C_2}{C_1'^2} - RT\,lnK$$

$$+ RT^2\left(\frac{2\,d\,ln\,C_1}{dT} + \frac{d\,ln\,C_2}{dT} - \frac{2\,d\,ln\,C'}{dT}\right)$$

$$- RT^2\frac{d\,lnK}{dT}$$

or

$$Q = RT^2\frac{d\,lnK}{dT}$$

$$- RT^2\left(\frac{2\,d\,ln\,C_1}{dT} + \frac{d\,ln\,C_2}{dT} - \frac{2\,d\,ln\,C'}{dT}\right);$$

but by equation (6)

$$\lambda - RT = RT^2\frac{d\,ln\,C}{dT};$$

and therefore

$$Q + 2(\lambda_1 - RT) + (\lambda_2 - RT)$$

$$- 2(\lambda' - RT) = RT^2\frac{d\,lnK}{dT},$$

in which λ_1, λ_2, λ' correspond respectively to H_2, O_2, H_2O. The expression on the left is nothing but the heat Q', developed by the formation of water in a homogeneous gaseous system.

This gives

$$(19) \qquad Q' = RT^2 \frac{d \ln K}{dT},$$

the equation of the reaction isochore.

In exactly the same manner we find in the most general case for the reaction

$$\nu_1 A_1 + \nu_2 A_2 + \cdots = \nu_1' A_1' + \cdots.$$

the corresponding equations

$$(20) \quad K = \frac{c_1^{\nu_1} c_2^{\nu_2} \cdots}{c_1'^{\nu_1'} \cdots} \text{ and } Q = RT^2 \frac{d \ln K}{dT}.$$

It may further be added that substances in condensed forms also can exist in the equilibrium box, and since no work is necessary to introduce or remove such forms, they may be disregarded in calculating A. This is simply stating the well-known fact that the active mass of a condensed form is constant (Guldberg).

Finally, for a gaseous system, if instead of the solid or liquid forms we take the substances in the gaseous form contained in large reservoirs, we obtain

$$(21) \quad A = -RT \ln K + RT \ln \frac{C_{0_1}{}^{\nu_1} C_{0_2}{}^{\nu_2} \ldots}{C_{0_1}'{}^{\nu_1'} \ldots}$$

in which the values of C_0 denote the concentrations of the gases in our reservoirs.*

Although it is not important for the purposes here in view, it may be remembered that according to the theory of van't Hoff these formulas hold good not only for gaseous systems but also for dilute solutions.

* For a further discussion of these relations consult Planck's "Thermodynamik" and the author's "Theoretical Chemistry."

LECTURE III

NEW EXPERIMENTAL RESEARCHES ON CHEMICAL EQUILIBRIA AT HIGH TEMPERATURES

THE formulas which we deduced in the last lecture have furnished the guiding principles for many experimental researches concerning chemical equilibria which have been carried on in recent times. In the hope of penetrating more deeply into the relations between chemical energy and heat, I have carried out in the last few years, together with my students, a number of investigations on reactions at high temperatures in gaseous systems, and I may perhaps be allowed to give here a brief account of this work.

I began by extending our methods for the determination of molecular weights to higher temperatures, using iridium vessels in the vapor density method of Victor Meyer. Heraeus in Hanau has been successful in recent years in working this material in a very skilful manner. For heating purposes I constructed an electric furnace, also of iridium. The limitations imposed by the great cost of iridium caused quite a number of changes to be made in the method used heretofore.

The details of the apparatus* can be seen in Figs. 2 and 3. Wide copper strips were fused to the iridium tube (furnace), the heating being effected by a current having an energy of 2000 to 3000 watts. By this means a temperature of 2000° could be attained and kept constant for a length of time sufficient to carry out a number of successive determinations. The tube was packed in burnt magnesia, which was in turn enclosed in an asbestos mantle, leaving access to the two ends. The lower end of the tube remained open to permit the temperature of the inner bulb to be determined by comparing the light radiated from it with the intensity of the radiation from a standardized luminous glower. The inner bulb, in which the substance under examination was vaporized, had the form of the usual Victor Meyer apparatus, but necessarily of much smaller dimensions. The upper part of the bulb was surrounded by a copper spiral through which water was made to circulate, and the substance was

* Nernst, Ztschr. f. Elektrochemie, 1903, 622.

retained in position there by means of the usual dropping device, till the bulb was heated to the required temperature. The substances were weighed and introduced into the bulb in small

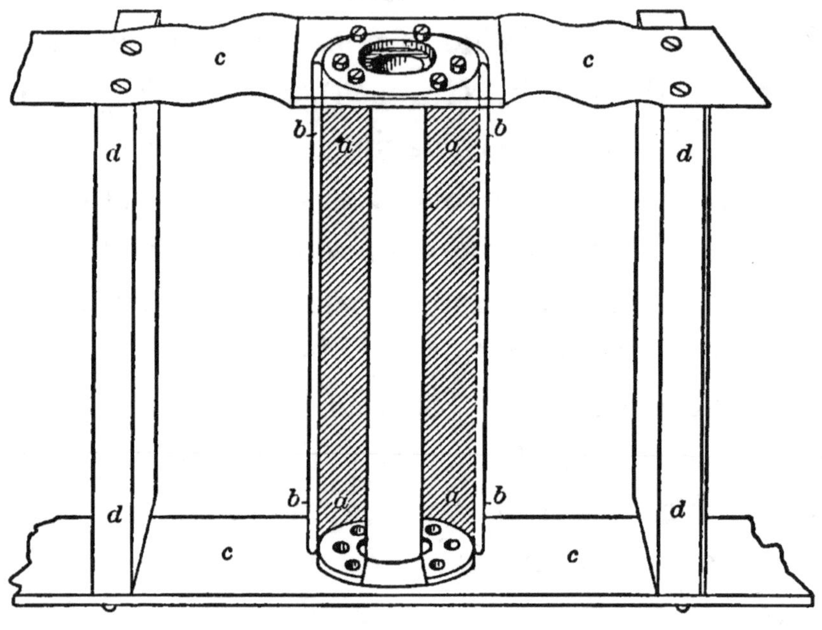

FIG. 2.

aa, Magnesia packing; bb, asbestos mantle; cc, electrodes; dd, wooden support (attached to wall not shown in the figure).

iridium vessels. The weighings, which were accurate to 0.001 to 0.002 mg. were made on a sensitive micro-balance, which I have described elsewhere. The volume of air displaced by the vaporization of the substance in the bulb was indicated by the motion of a drop of mercury in

a glass capillary connected to the bulb by a piece
of rubber tubing. This capillary was carefully
calibrated, and the increase in volume could thus
be determined with great accuracy.

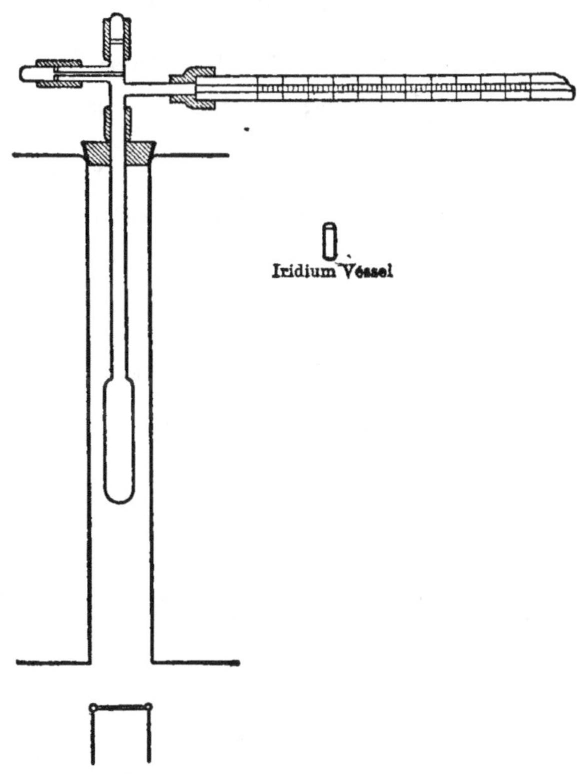

Fig. 3.

(One third actual size.)

Of the results obtained by the method described
above, the following may be mentioned: The
molecular weights of H_2O, CO_2, KCl, $NaCl$, SO_2,
were normal at temperatures of nearly 2000°;

sulphur was almost fifty per cent dissociated into atoms. Silver proved to be monatomic, as was to have been expected.*

For an exact determination of the degree of dissociation, and of chemical equilibria in general, the above method is unsuitable because the partial pressures in the Victor Meyer method cannot be accurately measured.† For this purpose a development of the "streaming method," first used by Deville, was found to be most suitable.

The mode of carrying out these experiments may be made clear by the accompanying sketch (Fig. 4).‡

FIG. 4.

The gaseous mixture to be studied is allowed to flow through a long tube. Between the points a and b the temperature t, at which the equilibrium is to be investigated, is maintained, while from

* Wartenberg, Berichte d. Deutsch. Chem. Gesell., **39**, 381.
† See, however, Loewenstein, Ztschr. f. phys. Chem., **54**, 711, who used a very ingenious modification.
‡ Cf. W. Nernst, Ztschr. f. anorg. Chem., **49**, 213.

b to c the temperature is made to fall as rapidly as possible, so that at c it has attained such a low value t' that the reaction velocity is practically zero. Evidently the following two conditions must be fulfilled in order that the gas leaving the tube shall have the same composition as at the equilibrium temperature: first, the distance ab must be sufficiently long to allow equilibrium to be attained; and secondly, the cooling space bc must be short enough not to change this equilibrium.

The first condition is fulfilled theoretically by making ab sufficiently long; practically this can best be done by widening the tube between a and b. In some cases a catalytic agent will answer the same purpose, the well-known investigations of Knietsch on the formation of sulphur trioxide being a good example of this. The question whether the reaction velocity is sufficiently large for the purpose at the temperature t, can be determined by passing through the tube mixtures whose composition is made to lie first on one side and then on the other of the composition of the equilibrium mixture.

The second condition is best fulfilled by making bc a narrow capillary in order to give as great a velocity as possible to the gaseous mixture, and to produce as large a fall in temperature as possible. It is, however, impossible to go beyond a certain limit here on account of the conductivity for heat of the material of the tube, and we consequently cannot conclude that this source of error has necessarily been avoided if the composition of the mixture leaving the apparatus is independent of the speed of the current of gas. This follows from the fact that an infinitely large velocity of the gas by no means necessitates an infinitely rapid fall in temperature. Substances acting catalytically must of course be excluded from bc.

Of especial importance is the fact that at high temperatures and correspondingly great reaction velocities, equilibrium is certainly reached in ab, but is just as certainly disturbed in bc. The gas leaving the apparatus will then have the same composition, no matter on which side of the equilibrium the composition of the original mixture lay, but in spite of this the final mixture may differ widely from the true composition of the equilibrium mixture.

The accompanying curves (Fig. 5) will perhaps show this more clearly; the unbroken curve is the equilibrium curve (showing percentages of the product of the reaction), while the dotted curve represents the observed values. In general, on account of the sources of error mentioned, the yield obtained will be too small. If, however, ab is long compared to bc, a region must always exist where correct values are obtained. The problem for the experimenter is to find the temperature

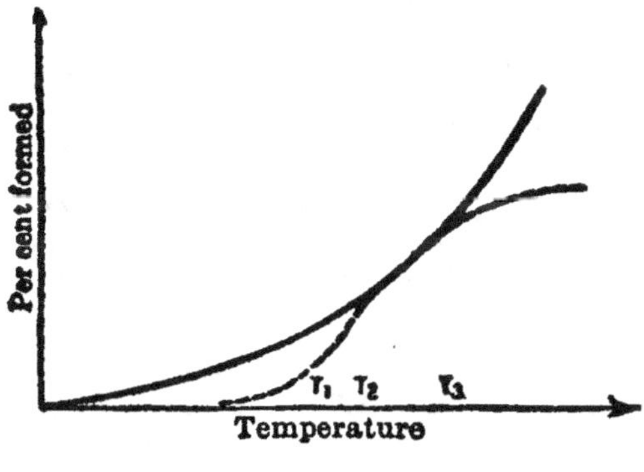

FIG. 5.

interval T_9 to T_9, within which the experimental values are correct, and which will evidently extend farther toward the left the greater the length of ab. A very important control in locating this region of correct experimental results is given by the fact that only within that region will the tangent of the observed curve coincide with that of the equilibrium curve, and since the latter can be calculated in most cases from the heat of reaction, we possess a trustworthy criterion as to whether the observed values in a given interval agree with the true values for the equilibrium.

In cases where, as in the neighborhood of T_9, the reaction velocity, although perceptible, is still too small for equilibrium to be attained in *ab* in the given time, it is possible by passing the gas mixtures through the tube at different rates to determine the two opposite reaction velocities, from which the concentration of the mixture at equilibrium can be calculated according to the principle of Guldberg and Waage, as was first pointed out by Dr. J. Sand,* in an investigation carried out in my laboratory.

Exactly the same observations apply to an entirely different kind of experiment. In the case of an explosion, the gaseous mixture is brought to a high temperature, remains at this temperature a very short time, and is then rapidly cooled. Since very small intervals of time are here involved, it is only in the regions of great reaction velocity that equilibrium will be reached—that is, at very high temperatures, where the method described above would wholly fail. In fact, a study of the explosion of mixtures of H_2, O_2, and atmos-

---

* J. Sand, Ztschr. f. phys. Chem., **50**, 465 (1904).

pheric air has proved that determinations of equilibria can be made at temperatures unattainable under other conditions. It is, of course, necessary in work of this kind to prove that the explosion temperature lies lower than T_3.

LECTURE IV

NEW EXPERIMENTAL RESEARCHES ON CHEMICAL EQUILIBRIA AT HIGH TEMPERATURES.—(*Concluded*).

In the last lecture it was pointed out that the attainment of equilibrium can be accelerated by means of catalysts.

The case is especially simple if, in the absence of a catalyst, the reaction takes place at only a very slow rate. It would then evidently suffice to place the catalyst in the space with the gas at the desired temperature, and to analyze the gas after a short time: the composition of the resulting mixture would correspond to the equilibrium at the temperature of the catalyst. The method is very simple when an electrically heated conductor, for example, a glowing platinum wire, has a sufficiently strong catalytic action. Wartenberg and I observed that it was possible to determine the dissociation of water vapor in this way. A glowing platinum wire in water vapor acts in such a way that after a time the water vapor is filled with the products of dissociation to an extent corresponding to the temperature of the platinum wire and the pressure of the water vapor. This method was worked out by Langmuir[*] in a recent investigation, in which the dissociation equilibria of H_2O and of CO_2 were determined very accurately.

A valuable indication of the reliability of the results obtained by the above methods may be derived from the law of mass action, by carrying out the experiments with suitable variations of the composition of the mixtures.

The great advantage of the streaming method described above consists in the possibility of simultaneously determining the reaction velocity. In this connection the work of my assistant, Jellinek,[†] on the velocity of formation and of decomposition of nitric oxide (NO), is worthy of special mention.

Finally, a very ingenious and simple method may be described, which was discovered and used for the first time by my pupil Loewenstein.[‡] In this method semipermeable membranes, whose theoretical importance was illustrated in the sec-

[*] I. Langmuir, J. Am. Chem., Soc. **28**, 1357.
[†] Jellinek, Ztschr. f. anorg. Chem., **49**, 229.
[‡] Loewenstein, Ztschr. f. phys. Chem., **54**, 715.

ond lecture, were put to practical use. Hydrogen, as is well known, diffuses through heated platinum and palladium, and as we found, also through iridium at very high temperatures. For utilizing this fact the following apparatus was constructed. (Fig. 6.)

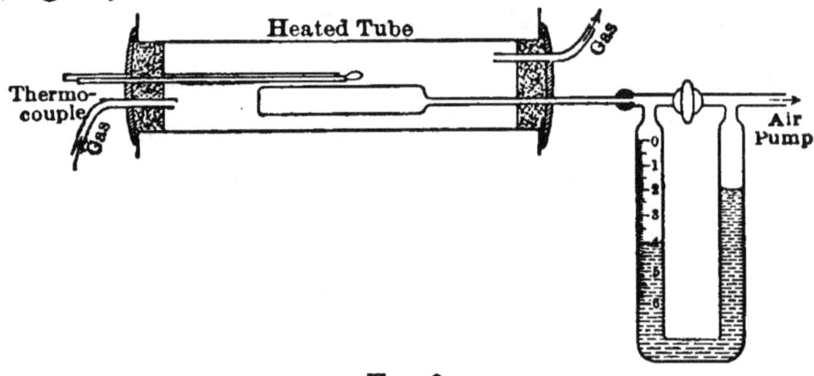

Fig. 6.

A platinum bulb 8 cm. long and 1.2 cm. in external diameter was connected by means of a capillary tube 12 cm. long and 0.5 mm. in diameter to an oil manometer and mercury air pump. The bulb was placed in the center of the horizontal tube, which was heated to the desired temperature, and water vapor, or any other gas which was to be examined, was passed through the tube. In carrying out a determination, the bulb was first evacuated, the oil in the two arms of the manometer brought to the same level by opening the stopcock shown in the figure and then closing it, and finally a regular stream of the gas whose dissociation was to be determined was passed through the tube while the latter was heated to a constant temperature. Hydrogen diffused through the walls of the bulb, and the vacuum above the arm of the manometer communicating with the pump being kept constant, the difference in level of the oil in the two arms gave the pressure of the hydrogen which had entered the bulb. After a few minutes this difference became constant and equal to the partial pressure of the hydrogen in the water vapor surrounding the bulb in the tube, and produced by the dissociation of the vapor. The temperature of the vapor in the tube was measured with the aid of a thermo-couple. By this method the dissociations of water vapor, hydrochloric acid, and hydrogen sulphide were measured.

In these experimental researches, which cover a period of about eight years, various forms of electric resistance furnaces were used. Besides those already described, two other forms may be mentioned.

(1) For temperatures up to 1000°, a copper tube coated with soapstone and water glass and wound with nickel wire allows a very uniform

temperature to be maintained within the tube, owing to the good conductivity of copper for heat.*

(2) In equilibria in which carbon takes part, an electric furnace of carbon permits of the employ-ment of very high temperatures. In this way Rothmund † in 1901 determined the equilibrium of the formation of calcium carbide.

Iridium when exposed to the air at high tem-peratures becomes disintegrated and crystalline on the surface, probably owing to the formation of a volatile oxide, stable only at high tempera-tures. To prevent this it was found best to coat the iridium used with a thin layer of oxides of zirconium and yttrium. The iridium for this purpose is painted with a solution of eighty per cent zirconium nitrate and twenty per cent yttrium nitrate and then heated to redness. This treat-ment is repeated twenty to thirty times. By quantitative measurements I was able to show that the loss of iridium when heated in air to about 2000° was very much decreased by this treatment.

For temperatures up to about 1650° a furnace

---

* Described for the first time by my pupil Hunter, Ztschr. f. phys. Chem., **53**, 441.

† Rothmund, Göttinger Nachrichten, 1901, Heft 3.

constructed of platinum exactly similar to the iridium furnace described is very durable and useful. A furnace of platinum with about twenty to thirty per cent iridium is available up to 1800°.

In the following tables, I and II, are given the results obtained for the technically important equilibria of the reactions

$$2NO = N_2 + O_2,$$

and

$$2H_2 + O_2 = 2H_2O.$$

TABLE I.—FORMATION OF NITRIC OXIDE

T	x (obs.)	x (calc.)	OBSERVER
1811	0.37	0.35	Nernst (l. c.).
1877	0.42	0.43	Nernst and Jellinek (l.c.).
2023	$0.52 < \ldots < 0.80$	0.64	" " " "
2033	0.64	0.67	Nernst (l. c.).
2195	0.97	0.98	" "
2580	2.05	2.02	Nernst and Finkh.*
2675	2.23	2.35	" " "

The last two values were obtained by the explosion method, the others by the streaming method. In the table x is the percentage by volume of NO formed in atmospheric air, the law of mass action furnishing therefore the relation

$$K = \frac{x^2}{\left(79.2 - \frac{x}{2}\right)\left(20.8 - \frac{x}{2}\right)}.$$

* Nernst and Finkh, Ztschr. f. anorg. Chem., **45** (1905), 116 and 126.

By integrating the equation of the reaction isochore, placing Q equal to 43200 independently of the temperature, we find

$$\log_{10} K = -\frac{43200}{4.571\,T} + \text{const.}$$

The agreement between the observed and calculated values for x is very satisfactory, as shown in the foregoing table, if we let

$$\text{const.} = 2\left[\log_{10} 0.0249 + 2.148\right] = 1.09.$$

TABLE II.—DISSOCIATION OF WATER VAPOR

T	x (obs.)	x (calc.)	OBSERVER
1300	0.0027	0.0029	Langmuir (l. c.).
1397	0.0078	0.0084	Nernst and Wartenberg.*
1480	0.0189	0.0185	" " "
1500	0.0197	0.0221	Langmuir (l. c.).
1561	0.034	0.0368	Nernst and Wartenberg.†
2155	1.18	1.18	Wartenberg. †
2257	1.77	1.79	"

The results of Nernst and Wartenberg were obtained by the streaming method, those of Wartenberg by the use of "semipermeable membranes" (iridium), and those of Langmuir by the catalytic action of a heated platinum wire.

* Nernst and Wartenberg, Ztschr. f. phys. Chem., **56**, 534.
† Wartenberg, Ztschr. f. phys. Chem., **56**, 513.

Since x denotes the percentage of dissociation, we have

$$c_1 = \frac{2Px}{RT(200+x)}, \quad c_2 = \frac{Px}{RT(200+x)},$$

$$c' = \frac{2P(100-x)}{RT(200+x)},$$

and therefore

$$K = \frac{P}{RT} \times \frac{x^3}{(200+x)(100-x)^2}.$$

If we take for the molecular heats * of H_2 and O_2

$$H_v = 4.68 + 0.00026\,T,$$

and for that of H_2O

$$H_v' = 5.61 + 0.000717\,T + 3.12\cdot10^{-7}T^2,$$

we obtain

$$Q' = 114400 + 2.74\,T - 0.00063\,T^2 - 6.24\cdot10^{-7}T^3$$

and hence, by integrating the equation of the reaction isochore,

$$\log \frac{2x^3}{\left(2+\dfrac{x}{100}\right)\left(1-\dfrac{x}{100}\right)^2} = 11.46 - \frac{25030}{T}$$

$$+ 2.38 \log \frac{T}{1000} - 1.38\cdot10^{-4}\,(T-1000)$$

$$- 0.685\cdot10^{-7}\,[T^2 - (1000)^2].$$

* Wartenberg, Verband. Deutsch. Phys. Gesell., **8**, 97 (1906).

The values calculated from this equation (given in the table under x (calc.)) show a very satisfactory agreement with the experimental data.

The above tables prove that the different methods employed give results which are in complete thermodynamic agreement, the differences being no greater than may be explained by the errors in the measurement of the temperatures. At the same time these tables represent the application of thermodynamics to gaseous systems at temperatures which are perhaps the highest at which such investigations have been carried out up to the present time.

In a similar manner a number of other reactions have been studied in my laboratory, among which the following may be mentioned:

$$2CO + O_2 = 2CO_2,*$$
$$N_2 + 2H_2O = 2NO + 2H_2,\dagger$$
$$O_2 + 4HCl = 2H_2O + 2Cl_2,$$
$$S_2 + C = CS_2.$$

* Nernst and Wartenberg, Ztschr. f. phys. Chem., **56, 548.**
† O. F. Tower, J. Am. Chem. Soc., **27,** 1209.

LECTURE V

INTEGRATION OF THE EQUATION OF THE REACTION ISOCHORE, PRELIMINARY DISCUSSION OF THE UNDETERMINED CONSTANT OF INTEGRATION, AND OF THE RELATION BETWEEN THE TOTAL AND THE FREE ENERGIES AT VERY LOW TEMPERATURES.

For the relation between chemical energy and heat development Berthelot, as is well known, believed he had found a very simple expression when he set the two magnitudes equal to each other. Closely connected with this question is the so-called "Thomson's Rule," proposed at an earlier date, according to which the electrical work furnished by a galvanic cell is equal to the heat developed by the chemical reaction producing the current.

We have seen, however, in a previous lecture, that there are formulas by means of which the maximum work of a reaction can be calculated with the aid of the constant K of the law of mass action, and when these were known it became possible to make an exact quantitative comparison between A and Q for a large number of chemical reactions. Another method was found in the calculation of A from the electromotive forces of such galvanic elements as are reversible, and therefore available for this purpose.[*]

It then became clear that the maximum work is not by any means equal to the heat effect determined thermochemically,—in fact, we can go a step further and say that it is often wholly illogical to compare these two quantities directly with each other.

The heat (Q) developed, for example, in the formation of water vapor from gaseous hydrogen and oxygen, is independent of the concentrations of the reacting substances, but the maximum work (A) given by the formula already derived

$$(21) \qquad A = - RT \ln K + RT \ln \frac{C_{0_1}'^{\nu_1} \, C_{0_2}'^{\nu_2} \, \ldots}{C_{0_1}''^{\nu_1'} \, \ldots}$$

depends on the concentrations of both the reacting substances and of the water vapor formed. We can therefore let A assume any magnitude we choose by suitably varying the concentra-

---

[*] Cf. Nernst, "Theoretical Chemistry" (English translation of the fourth German edition), p. 685 ff. and p. 712 ff.

tions, whereas Q always retains the same value. Further, if we consider our fundamental formula

$$A - Q = T\frac{dA}{dT},$$

and if, according to the principle proposed by Berthelot, $A = Q$ at all temperatures, then both A and Q must be independent of the temperature. The constancy of Q would require the existence of certain relations, already explained, between the specific heats of the substances taking part in the reaction, but experiment has shown that in general these conditions are not fulfilled.

Upon attempting to find the mathematical relations between A and Q it can easily be seen that A cannot be calculated from Q by means of the two laws of thermodynamics, for if

$$A = f(T)$$

were a solution of our fundamental formula, then

$$A = f(T) + a'T,$$

in which a' is an absolutely indefinite constant, would be a solution also.

We have therefore arrived at the two following results, which must be stated before any further development of the theory can be attempted.

(1) The relation

$$A = Q$$

is contrary to the results of experiment, and is often hardly logical.

(2) The principles of thermodynamics do not enable us to find the relation between A and Q; i. e., to calculate a chemical equilibrium from the heat of reaction.

Moreover, the correctness of the second statement can be clearly shown by integrating the equation of the reaction isochore. By combining equations (16) and (19) we find

$$(22) \quad lnK = -\frac{Q_0'}{RT} + \frac{\Sigma\nu a}{R}ln\,T + \frac{\Sigma\nu\beta}{R}T$$
$$+\cdots+I,$$

in which I is a constant of integration whose value is thus far entirely undetermined. Therefore if a new law of thermodynamics is to be found, it is clear from the outset that it must concern the above constant of integration as the only remaining problem.

Can we hope to derive such a law? I have thought for a long time that this question was to be answered affirmatively. In the different editions of my "Theoretical Chemistry" I have stated that in the Principle of Berthelot, even if it is incorrect in the form used up to the present, there lies hidden a law of nature, the further development of which seems to be of the greatest importance.

To enable us to proceed it is necessary to find the conditions under which the Principle of Berthelot comes nearest to expressing the true relation between chemical energy and heat, or, what amounts to the same thing, between the magnitudes A and Q. In this direction we can show that in' reactions between solids, liquids, or concentrated solutions the values of A and Q approach each other very closely, while on the other hand, in dilute solutions or with gases we usually find large differences between the two quantities; but in these latter cases, as we have seen already, the comparison is not permissible on account of the nature of the formulas.

As examples illustrating the facts, let us compare the electromotive forces of some galvanic cells with the heats developed by the chemical reactions taking place in them.

TABLE A

CHEMICAL REACTION	A	Q
$2Hg + PbCl_2 = Pb + 2HgCl$	0.54	0.44
$2Ag + PbCl_2 = Pb + 2AgCl$	0.49	0.52
$2Ag + I_2 = 2AgI$	0.68	0.60
$Pb + I_2 = PbI_2$	0.89	0.87

In the table A and Q are both expressed in volts. Similarly, the electromotive force of the well-known lead storage cell, when concentrated sulphuric acid is used, is almost exactly equal to the thermochemical energy.

Further, Bodländer* found in 1898 that he could calculate the solubility of salts from their heats of formation and their decomposition potentials, and he pointed out very clearly that the agreement between the experimental and the calculated solubilities was satisfactory only when the decomposition products of the electrolysis were solid substances. Silver iodide (AgI) may be mentioned as an example.

Furthermore, I found in 1894† in comparing the change in total energy with that of free energy, or in other words the heat of reaction with the osmotic work, in concentrated solutions of sulphuric acid, that these two magnitudes are nearly equal to each other, whereas in dilute solutions the difference is very great.

But even in the cases mentioned above, there is no doubt that the principle of the equality of A and Q at ordinary temperatures, is far from an

* Bodländer, Ztschr. f. phys. Chem., **27**, 55.
† Nernst, Wiedemann's Annalen, **53**, 57.

exact law. Not only do the differences between A and Q exceed the errors of observation, but the consideration of the physico-chemical process of fusion also proves in a most striking manner that A and Q can differ very greatly, even when only solids and liquids take part in the transformation. In fact at the melting point, A is almost exactly zero, whereas Q, the latent heat of fusion, has a considerable value.

A long study of this relation in past years has led me to the hypothesis that *we are dealing with a law more or less approximate at ordinary temperatures, but true in the neighborhood of absolute zero.*

That A and Q are exactly equal at the absolute zero is a necessary consequence of the fundamental formula

$$A - Q = T\frac{dA}{dT},$$

when Q, and therefore also A, is supposed to be a continuous function of T down to absolute zero; but what I should like to point out is that A and Q are not only equal to each other at the absolute zero, but also that their values coincide completely in the immediate vicinity of this point. To illustrate graphically, the curves for Q and A (Fig. 7), not only terminate in the same point at absolute zero (cf. I), but are also tangent to each other (cf. II).

I was very much surprised, in following up the consequences of this hypothesis, to find that it contains the solution of the problem concerning the

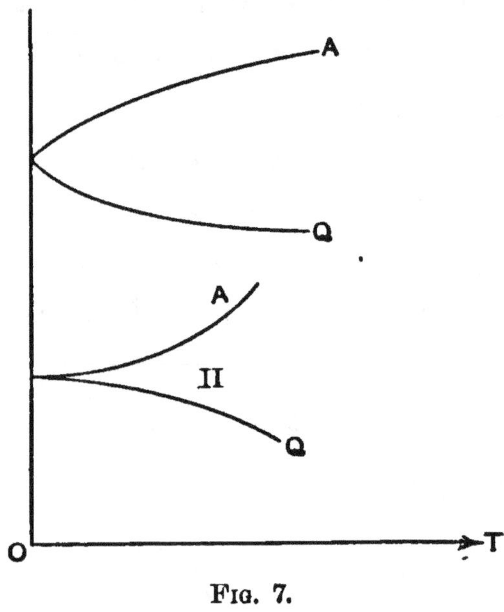

Fig. 7.

relations between the chemical affinity A, and Q the heat developed. The consideration of these consequences and the calculation of practical examples will form the subject of the following lectures.

We must not forget that we are here dealing with a hypothesis which we cannot verify directly, because we are unable to measure Q and A at temperatures in the vicinity of the absolute zero. It is clear, however, that a knowledge of specific heats down to absolute zero would enable us to undertake an accurate test of our hypothesis, but even if these values are not known, we can in many cases extrapolate with sufficient accuracy to furnish an adequate confirmation.

To apply our hypothesis, let us consider a reaction

$$n_1 a_1 + n_2 a_2 + \cdots = n_1' a_1' + n_2' a_2' + \cdots$$

between solid and liquid substances only. According to our previous assumption we set

$$(22a) \qquad Q = Q_0 + aT + bT^2 + cT^3 + \cdots,$$

in which the coefficients a, b, c, ... are to be calculated from the specific heats.

$$a = \Sigma n \alpha_0, \quad b = \Sigma n \beta_0, \text{ etc.}$$

We shall attempt, *by means of the additional hypothesis** that A, like Q, may be expressed by a series containing only integral powers of T, to determine whether*

$$(23) \qquad A = A_0 + a'T + b'T^2 + c'T^3 + \cdots$$

---

* Such hypotheses are usual in thermodynamics and other branches of theoretical physics, but it does not seem to be customary to point out that such expansions into series are hypothetical and are only to be justified by experimental investigations.

represents a correct solution of our fundamental formula

$$A - Q = T \frac{dA}{dT}.$$

We find by substitution

$$A_0 - Q_0 + (a' - a) T + (b' - b) T^2 + (c' - c) - T^3$$
$$+ \cdots\cdots = a' T + 2 b' T^2 + 3 c' T^3 + \cdots\cdots,$$

and since the last equation must hold at all temperatures, the relations

$$A_0 = Q_0, \quad a' - a = a', \quad b' - b = 2 b',$$
$$c' - c = 3 c', \quad \text{etc.,}$$

follow as necessary and sufficient conditions, from which we obtain

$$(24) \quad A_0 = Q_0, \ a = 0, \ b = -b', \ c = -2c', \ \text{etc.}$$

The second law of thermodynamics requires then (upon the above very probable assumption that both A and Q may be expressed by development into series containing only integral powers of T), that at absolute zero A, the chemical affinity, must be equal to Q, the heat developed, and further that

$$a = \Sigma n \, a_0 = 0.$$

That is, the specific heats are additive at absolute zero, a relation which has been found to be approximately true for solid bodies at ordinary temperatures. For liquids the law does not hold even approximately at ordinary temperatures, and I think the explanation for this fact is simply that the specific heats of liquids increase much more rapidly with rise in temperature than those of solids.

The essential point of our new hypothesis

$$(25) \qquad lim. \frac{dA}{dT} = \frac{dQ}{dT} \quad \text{when} \quad T=0,$$

can now be expressed very concisely by the equation

$$(26) \qquad a' = 0.$$

If we do not wish to make the hypothesis that A may be expressed by development into a series containing only integral powers of T_s it would be easy to integrate equations (1) and (22a), obtaining thereby the following equation:

$$A \doteq Q_0 + a'T - aT \ln T - bT^2 - \frac{c}{2}T^3 - \ldots .$$

From the hypothesis

$$lim. \left(\frac{dQ}{dT} = a + 2bT + \ldots . = \frac{dA}{dT} = a' - a \right.$$

$$\left. - a \ln T - 2bT - \ldots . \right) \quad \text{when} \quad T = 0,$$

the same result follows as before, namely,

$$a = 0 \quad \text{and} \quad a' = 0.$$

The simplest application of the above formulas would be the calculation of the electromotive force of the galvanic cells which we considered on p. 43, from the heats of reaction and the specific heats. In fact we find *

$$A = nE\,23046 = Q_0 - T^2 \Sigma n \beta_0 + \cdots,$$

from which E can be calculated in volts if the heats of reaction are expressed in gram calories per n electrochemical equivalents. But since the experimental data are not sufficient for an exact test of the above relation, we shall consider here only the simple equilibrium

$$\underset{\text{(liquid)}}{a} = \underset{\text{(solid)}}{a'},$$

that is, the process of solidification.

The maximum work which can be gained by this reaction is

$$A = RT ln \frac{C}{C'},$$

where C and C' denote the concentrations of saturated vapor at the temperature T. Our theory requires that

$$A = Q_0 - (\beta_0 - \beta_0')\,T^2 - \frac{(\gamma_0 - \gamma_0')}{2}\,T^3 - \cdots.$$

* With regard to the numerical factor in this equation, cf. the author's " Theoretical Chemistry," p. 703, and also Ztschr. f. Elektrochemie, **10,** 629 (1904).

If the molecular heat of the liquid is

$$h_0 = a_0 + 2\beta_0 T + 3\gamma_0 T^2 + \cdots,$$

and that of the solid

$$h_0' = a_0 + 2\beta_0' T + 3\gamma_0' T^2 + \cdots.$$

the latent heat of fusion will be

$$Q = Q_0 + (\beta_0 - \beta_0') T^2 + (\gamma - \gamma_0') T^3 + \cdots$$

The melting point T_s is determined by the condition,

$$A = 0 = Q_0 - (\beta_0 - \beta_0') T_0^2 - \frac{(\gamma_0 - \gamma_0')}{2} T_0^3 - \cdots$$

or, by disregarding the higher terms,

$$(27) \qquad T_0^2 = \frac{Q_0}{\beta_0 - \beta_0'}.$$

If we introduce the molecular heats at the melting point,

$$H_0 = a_0 + 2\beta_0 T_0 \quad \text{and} \quad H_0' = a_0 + 2\beta_0' T_0,$$

it follows that

$$(28) \qquad T_0 = \frac{2Q_0}{H_0 - H_0'} = \frac{\sigma}{H_0 - H_0'},$$

in which σ denotes the heat of fusion at the melting point T_s, and therefore

$$\sigma = Q_0 + (\beta_0 - \beta_0') T_0^2 = 2Q_0.$$

Our theory allows us, therefore, to calculate the melting points from thermal magnitudes only, and if it were justifiable to assume that the specific heats for the liquid and solid states increase linearly with the temperature, the melting points could be found by dividing the molecular heat of fusion by the difference between the molecular heats of the solid and liquid forms at the melting point. Indeed Tammann in his admirable work, "Krystallisieren und Schmelzen," Leipzig, 1903, p. 42, showed, from the empirical side, that this relation holds true in many cases. Evidently it is not always permissible to disregard the higher powers of T. It would be almost hopeless to attempt a direct experimental verification, because the undercooling of the liquid below the solidification temperature which would be necessary in order to determine the specific heats at very low temperatures, would be impossible; but perhaps we may hope to find a theoretical method which will enable us to determine these values.

We are thus able to prove in qualitative agreement with our hypothesis, that the specific heat of a substance is always greater in the liquid than in the solid state; otherwise an equilibrium, that is, a melting point, could not exist,—at least not at the pressure of the saturated vapor.

LECTURE VI

DETERMINATION AND EVALUATION OF THE CONSTANT OF INTEGRATION BY MEANS OF THE CURVE OF VAPOR PRESSURE

AMONG the relations deduced in the second lecture we found, for a reaction

$$n_1 a_1 + n_2 a_2 + \cdots = n_1' a_1' + \cdots.$$

the two equations

$$Q = Q_0' + \Sigma n\, a_0 T + \Sigma n \beta_0 T^2 + \cdots$$

and

$$A = RT \ln \frac{C_1^{n_1} C_2^{n_2} \cdots}{C_1'^{\,n_1'} \cdots} - RT \ln K.$$

Substituting in the latter from equation (13) the expression for the concentrations of saturated vapor

$$\ln C = -\frac{\lambda_0}{RT} + \frac{a - a_0}{R} \ln T + \frac{\beta - \beta_0}{R} T + \cdots + i,$$

and from equation (22) the expression for the equilibrium of a homogeneous gaseous system

$$\ln K = -\frac{Q_0'}{RT} + \frac{\Sigma \nu a}{R} \ln T + \frac{\Sigma \nu \beta}{R} T + \cdots + I,$$

we find, since $\quad Q_0 = Q_0' - \Sigma \nu \lambda_0,$

$$A = Q_0 + (\Sigma n i - I)RT - \Sigma n \alpha_0 \cdot T \ln T - \Sigma n \beta_0 \cdot T^2.$$

By comparison with equation (24) we obtain

$$a = \Sigma n \alpha_0 = 0, \quad \text{and} \quad a' = \Sigma (n i - I) R = 0.$$

The constant of integration I, which as we have seen is not determinable by the second law of thermodynamics, is therefore given according to our theory by the equation

$$(29) \qquad\qquad I = \Sigma n i.$$

That is, the constant I is referred to a sum of constants of integration i which are peculiar to each individual substance, and can be found by separate measurements carried out on every substance.

We have found further that by equation (24)

$$b = -b',$$

and also that $\qquad b = + \Sigma n \beta_0.$

Hence $\qquad\qquad b' = -\Sigma n \beta_0.$

It is historically worthy of note that Boltzmann [*] in 1882 pointed out that a kinetic treatment of gaseous equilibrium should theoretically lead us farther than could the application of the principles of thermodynamics, but no new results of practical value have as yet been found in this way.

After having finished the above calculations I

---

[*] Boltzmann, Wiedemann's Annalen, **22**, 64.

found in the monograph of Le Chatelier, "Recherches sur les équilibres chimiques "* (1888), a passage where in speaking of a formula analogous to equation (22), the author makes the following statement:

"It is very probable that the constant of integration like the coefficients of the differential equation is a definite function of certain physical properties of the reacting substances. The determination of the nature of this function would lead to a complete knowledge of the laws of equilibrium; it would make it possible to determine, *a priori*, all the conditions of equilibrium relating to a given chemical reaction without the addition of new experimental data. The exact nature of this constant has not been determined up to the present time."

In these words the renowned French chemist not only formulated the problem under discussion in a very exact manner, but he seems also to have had some idea of the method for its solution (see page 204).† For my part I should like to add that the new theorem used by me, and which, as I believe I have shown, leads to the solution of the

---

* Also printed in Annales des mines (mémoires), ser. 8, vol. **13.** See page 336.

† Corresponding to Annales des mines (mémoires), ser. 8, vol. **13,** page 356.

problem, will perhaps prove fruitful in other branches of science (theory of mixtures, theory of radiation, etc.).

In 1902 a very interesting paper was published by T. W. Richards * on "The relation of changing heat capacity to change of free energy, heat of reaction, change of volume, and chemical affinity," in which he pointed out very clearly that the question whether $A > Q$ or $Q > A$ above absolute zero (where $A = Q$), depends upon whether the heat capacity is increased or decreased by the chemical process, and I am very glad to be able to state that our formulas agree qualitatively in many cases with the conclusions of Richards. I do not wish to enter here into a discussion of the differeuces in the quantitative relations.

The point of view taken by van't Hoff in the "Boltzmann Festschrift" (1904) in following up the conclusions of Richards, tends qualitatively in a somewhat similar direction, but quantitatively is very different.

Furthermore, I wish to mention the fact that Haber, in his remarkable book "Thermodynamik technischer Gasreaktionen" (which appeared re-

---

* T. W. Richards, Proceedings of the American Academy of Arts and Sciences, **38**, 293.

cently), also clearly formulated the problem under discussion and, at any rate in some cases, attempted its solution. His deductions, however, appear to me to differ from mine in important points; in particular, in that the integration constant according to my formulas does not become zero, as Haber considers it may, for gaseous reactions in which the number of molecules remains unaltered. Haber, however, fully recognized the importance of specific heats for the further development of thermodynamics.

The most important problem appears to be the numerical evaluation of the integration constant i. After having solved this problem, we shall be able to test our hypothesis directly by calculating the equilibria of gaseous systems. In the second lecture we deduced the equation (13),

$$ln\,C = -\frac{\lambda_0}{RT} + \frac{a-a_0}{R}\,ln\,T + \frac{\beta-\beta_0}{R}\,T + \cdots + i.$$

By introducing the vapor pressure p according to the formula

$$p = CRT,$$

we obtain

$$(30) \quad ln\,p = -\frac{\lambda_0}{RT} + \frac{R+a-a_0}{R}\,ln\,T$$
$$+ \frac{\beta-\beta_0}{R}\,T + i + ln\,R.$$

My first plan was to use for this purpose the theorem of corresponding states, according to which the equation

$$\frac{p}{\pi} = f\left(\frac{T}{\tau}\right),$$

in which π is the critical pressure and τ the critical temperature, must hold for all substances. In this equation $f\left(\frac{T}{\tau}\right)$ is a function of the temperature, independent of the nature of the substance in question. As an approximation formula, van der Waals derived the following:

$$(31) \qquad \log\frac{\pi}{p} = a\left(\frac{\tau}{T} - 1\right),$$

or

$$(31a) \qquad \log p = -a\,\frac{\tau}{T} + a + \log\pi,$$

in which a should have a value constant for all substances. Van der Waals found this value to be about 3.0.

Unfortunately the theorem of corresponding states is very far from being true, as has been pointed out by several authors, and this I wish to illustrate by the accompanying curves (Fig. 8), in plotting which the latest determinations for hydrogen, argon, etc., have been used. It is advanta-geons to plot as abscissas the values of $\left(\dfrac{\tau}{T}-1\right)$, and as ordinates the values of $\log\dfrac{\pi}{p}$, as has been

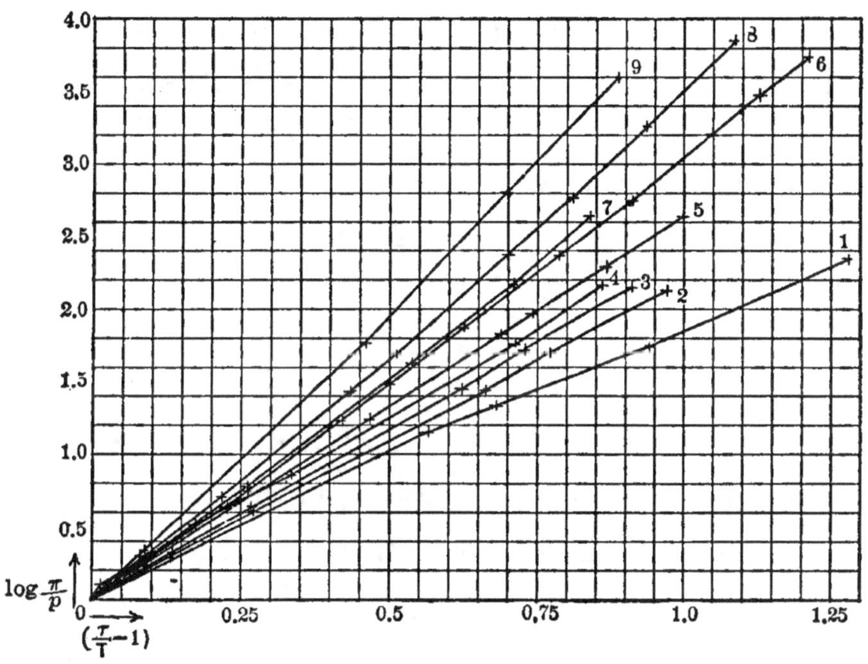

Fig. 8.

1. Hydrogen.
2. Argon.
3. Krypton.
4. Oxygen.
5. Carbon bisulphide.

6. Phenyl fluoride.
7. Ether.
8. Propyl acetate.
9. Ethyl alcohol.

done in the above figure. Although we obtain from the formula (31a)

$$\log p = -a\,\frac{\tau}{T} + a + \log \pi$$

curves which are almost straight lines, these curves not only do not coincide, but obviously diverge more and more as they approach absolute zero. We are forced therefore to give up this method, but not without having proved that the vapor pressure curves, even if not coincident, are still similar and would not intersect each other.[*]

Adopting now the thermodynamic method we may recall equation (30)

$$ln\,p = -\frac{\lambda_0}{RT} + \frac{R + a - a_0}{R}\,ln\,T$$

$$+ \frac{\beta - \beta_0}{R}\,T + i + ln\,R,$$

to which, as has been stated, the gas laws are supposed to be applicable. Unfortunately the range of temperature within which the gas laws hold for the saturated vapor, and where we have experimental data applicable to the above formula, is small, and it is therefore impossible to determine the coefficients λ_0, a, b, ..., i, even with a moderate degree of accuracy. It consequently seems desirable to fill this experimental deficiency by continuing the vapor pressure curves as far as possible in the direction of very small pressures, for example to 0.001 mm. of mercury,

*Bingham, J. Am. Chem. Soc., **28**, 717.

and I have begun to work in this direction in my laboratory.

From examination of equation (30) it would not appear very probable that the curves drawn in the figure would be so nearly straight lines as the experimental data show, and as equation (31a) requires. Since without doubt the first members are the most important, partial mutual compensation is to be expected, that is, the coefficients a and b must have opposite signs. Since at ordinary temperatures, the specific heat of the liquid is always greater than that of the saturated vapor, at very low temperatures the specific heat of the saturated vapor must conversely be greater than that of the liquid.

This conclusion, drawn from the form of the vapor pressure curves, is justified by applying the kinetic theory of gases. According to this theory, for a monatomic gas the molecular heat at constant pressure, H_p, must be equal to 5.0 at all temperatures, and the molecular heats of polyatomic gases must always be greater than 5.0; whereas the molecular heats of liquid or solid bodies as given by the latest measurements at low temperatures, diminish very rapidly with the temperature. By examining the experimental data and by calculating a large number of vapor pressure curves, I arrived finally at the following conclusions:

(1) The molecular heats of gases at constant pressure near absolute zero—at absolute zero itself, of course, a gas cannot exist and must be a con-densed crystallized or amorphous body—can be expressed by

$$(32) \qquad H_p^0 = 3.5 + m \times 1.5,$$

in which m denotes the number of atoms in each molecule of the gas.

According to this equation the molecular heats of the monatomic gases,

$$H_p^0 = 3.5 + 1.5 = 5.0,$$

are in agreement with the kinetic theory.

For diatomic gases we have

$$H_p^0 = 3.5 + 2 \times 1.5 = 6.5,$$

whereas by extrapolation of Langen's * measure-ments for O_2, H_2, N_2, CO, and for which he gave the expression

$$H_p^t = 6.8 + 0.0012t,$$

we do in fact obtain for $T = 0$ or $t = -273$

$$H_p^0 = 6.5.$$

The extrapolation of the new measurements of Holborn and Austin † for CO_2 and of Holborn

* Langen, Ztschr. d. Vereins deutscher Ingenieure, **47**, 637.

† Holborn and Austin, Sitzungsber. d. K. Akad. d. Wissensch., Berlin, p. 175 (1905).

and Hemming * for H_2O gives

$$H_p^0 = 7.3 \text{ for } CO_2; \quad H_p^0 = 7.6 \text{ for } H_2O,$$

which seem to agree sufficiently well, considering the large extrapolations, with the value 8.0 calculated from equation (32).

Other measurements as well, perhaps hardly accurate enough for extrapolation, appear not to contradict this formula.

(2) For the specific heats of liquids or solids at the absolute zero, our hypothesis requires that every atom shall have a definite value for the atomic heat, independent of the form, crystallized or liquid (i. e., amorphous), and of whether it is in chemical combination with other atoms.

Numerous measurements by different experimenters have shown, in full agreement with each other, that the atomic heats in the solid state decrease greatly at low temperatures, but at the present time it is impossible to calculate the limiting value toward which they tend. For want of a better assumption I believe we can set for the present the value of the atomic heats at absolute zero for all elements equal to 1.5. Of course it is somewhat unsatisfactory to calculate with such a doubtful value; but on the one hand

* Holborn and Hemming, Drude's Ann., **18**, 739.

we are obliged for the sake of the following calculations to make some assumption, and on the other hand it makes little difference for the following purposes what value the atomic heat has between the limits 0 and 2. That the atomic heats, however, do sink to such small values for the elements like H, C, N, S, O, Cl, is unquestionable. It is with the compounds of these elements that we shall be concerned in our subsequent calculations.

By combining the two statements we find that near absolute zero the molecular heat of the vapor at constant pressure would exceed the molecular heat of the condensed product by an amount equal to 3.5 gram calories. This statement seems to me not improbable from the point of view of the kinetic theory.

(3) The theorem of corresponding states, which we find to be very far removed from the truth when applied to vapor pressures, agrees very satisfactorily, as Young* has shown, for the volume relations. Young states in particular that the volumes of the saturated vapors of the substances investigated by him have almost identical values at corresponding pressures. I found as a very simple empirical function the equation

* Young, Phil. Mag. [5], **34**, 505.

$$(33) \qquad p(v - v') = RT\left(1 - \frac{p}{\pi}\right),$$

in which v denotes the molecular volume of the vapor, v', that of the liquid, p the pressure of the vapor, and π the critical pressure.

The following table (III) shows the range of its accuracy for phenyl fluoride (C_6H_5F) which Young * used as his standard substance.

TABLE III

T	p	v	v'	$\dfrac{p(v-v')}{T}$	$R\left(1 - \dfrac{p}{\pi}\right)$
small	small	large	small	0.0821	0.0821
367.3	1.316	22.00	0.103	0.0786	0.0796
435.0	6.580	4.634	0.115	0.0684	0.0700
473.6	13.16	2.265	0.125	0.0593	0.0579
519.7	26.32	1.009	0.145	0.0438	0.0337
550.0	39.5	0.516	0.179	0.0242	0.0094
559.6	44.6	0.270	0.270	0.000	0.000

The formula can therefore be employed up to rather high pressures if we accept the above statement of Young as holding true in all cases.

The heat of vaporization can also be expressed by the formula

$$(34) \qquad \lambda = (\lambda_0 + 3.5\,T - \epsilon\,T^2)\left(1 - \frac{p}{\pi}\right).$$

An experimental verification of this formula will

* Loc. cit.

be given later; if we introduce these two last equations in the equation of Clausius-Clapeyron

$$\lambda = T\frac{dp}{dT}(v - v'),$$

we have

$$RT^2\frac{d\,lnp}{dT} = \lambda_0 + 3.5\,T - \epsilon\,T^2,$$

whose integral is

$$(35)\quad lnp = -\frac{\lambda_0}{RT} + \frac{3.5}{R}\,ln\,T - \frac{\epsilon}{R}\,T + i + ln\,R,$$

adopting the same notation for the integration constant as in equation (30).

Since equations (33) and (34), though not valid up to the critical point, do nevertheless hold up to a point fairly close to it, it is clear that the integration of equation (35) with the critical point as one of the limits of integration will give an equation which will not be without its uses.

For the desired integration constant i, or, more simply, for the value of C as used in the following discussion, equation (35) gives us

$$(36)\quad C = \frac{i + ln\,R}{2.3023} = \frac{\lambda_0}{4.571\,T_1} - 1.75\log T_1$$
$$+ \frac{\epsilon}{4.571}\,T_1 + \log p_1.$$

The following data are therefore necessary:

(1) A point in the vapor pressure curve p_1, T_1.

(2) The value of $\dfrac{d\lambda}{dT}$ for $T = T_1$ (for the calculation of ϵ).*

(3) The value of the heat of vaporization λ_1 corresponding to the temperature T_1 (for the calculation of λ according to formula (34)).

(4) An approximate value for the critical pressure.

* By differentiating equation (34), noting that $\dfrac{p}{\pi}$ is small in comparison to 1, we find $\epsilon = \dfrac{1}{2T_1}\left(3.5 - \dfrac{d\lambda}{dT} + \dfrac{\lambda_1 \lambda_0}{RT_1^2}\cdot\dfrac{p_1}{\pi}\right)$.

LECTURE VII

DETERMINATION AND EVALUATION OF THE CONSTANT OF INTEGRATION BY MEANS OF THE CURVE OF VAPOR PRESSURE.— (*Concluded*)

As an example of the method of calculating C let us consider the case of ammonia, which has been studied very thoroughly by Dieterici.* Placing $p = 4.21$ atmospheres, $T = 273$, $\lambda = 5265$, $\pi = 113$ atmospheres, we find

$$\epsilon T = 7.6, \quad \lambda_0 = 6580,$$

and consequently, from equation (36),

$$C = 3.28$$

A further control of the value of ϵ, and, in general, of the reliability of this method of calculation, is obtained from equation (34),

$$\lambda = (\lambda_0 + 3.5\,T - \epsilon\,T^2)\left(1 - \frac{p}{\pi}\right).$$

Substituting in this the above values

$$\lambda_0 = 6580, \quad \epsilon = 0.02785, \quad \pi = 113,$$

* Dieterici, Ztschr. für Kälteindustrie, 1904.

we obtain the values given in the following table:

TABLE IV

p	T	λ (calc.)	λ (obs.)
4.2	273.	(5260)	(5260)
8.5	293.	4820	4850
15.5	313.	4270	4390
25.8	333.	3590	3870
48.3	363.	2390	2940

As the table shows, equation (34) has a validity similar to that of equation (33), that is, it holds up to pressures of about 20 atmospheres. The values given under λ (obs.) are the heats of vaporization which were found by Dieterici in the investigation already quoted.

Last summer, Dr. Brill* measured with the greatest care the vapor pressures of liquid ammonia down to the melting point. In the following table, the observed values are given together with those calculated according to equation (36), which becomes

$$\log p = -\frac{6580}{4.571\,T} + 1.75 \log T - \frac{0.02785\,T}{4.571} + C.$$

* Brill, Ann. der Physik, [4] 21, 170.

TABLE V

T	p (mm. Hg) (obs.)	p (calc.)
195.4	44.1	43.9
200.3	62.5	64.7
204.7	87.5	90.8
210.2	136.0	133.9
216.5	210.0	204.6
222.3	309.3	294.1
228.0	437.1	411.5
234.8	610.4	599.2
240.0	761.0	787.0

In calculating p the empirical value

$$C = 3.31,$$

was used, which is in very satisfactory agreement with the value found above,

$$C = 3.28.$$

By calculating a number of examples I found that we can set with sufficient accuracy

$$(37) \qquad -\frac{d\lambda}{dT} = h_0 - H_p^0,$$

h_0 being the molecular heat of the liquid at T. This equation, moreover, must be the more exact the lower the temperature. Combining, further, equations (32), (36), and (37), we obtain

$$(38) \quad C = \frac{1}{4.571}\left(\frac{\lambda_1}{\left(1 - \frac{p_1}{\pi}\right) T_1} + h_0 - m \cdot 1.5 - 3.5 \right)$$
$$+ \log p_1 - 1.75 \log T_1.$$

The experimental data necessary for the application of (38) are more easily obtained than those required in order to apply (36).

In Table VI are given the values of C for various liquids, calculated according to formula (38). The following table (VIa) contains the values for oxygen and nitrogen, which are calculated in exactly the same way as was done in the case of ammonia, using the experimental data recently published by Alt.*

TABLE VI

'Substance	T_1	p_1	$\dfrac{\lambda_1}{1 - \dfrac{p}{\pi}}$	h_0	C
Sulphur dioxide....	273.	1.53	6000	20.3	3.42
Carbon bisulphide..	273.	0.168	6766	17.9	3.26
Chloroform	313.	0.487	7490	28.3	4.07
Ethyl ether........	273.	0.244	6919	39.1	3.56
Benzol	293.	0.099	8142	32.2	3.12
Alcohol	303.	0.103	10100	28.5	4.48
Water.............	273.	0.0060	10670	18.0	4.26

* Alt, Abh. d. Bayr. Acad. d. Wiss., II Kl., **22** (1905).

TABLE VIa

SUBSTANCE	T_1	p_1	$\dfrac{\lambda_1}{1-\dfrac{p}{\pi}}$	$-\dfrac{d\lambda}{dT}$	λ_0	C
O_2............	78	0.24	1740	6.7	1826	2.20
N_2............	68	0.26	1470	7.7	1572	2.37

It may be hoped that these values of C are at least approximately correct. A support for their correctness is the fact that the calculation of C from equation (38), which for sufficiently small vapor pressures is directly applicable to the solid state, gives similar values. This is shown in Table VII, for which the heat of vaporization of iodine was calculated from its vapor pressure, and the value of λ_1 for the other two substances by the addition of the molecular heat of fusion to the heat of vaporization as calculated above.

TABLE VII

SUBSTANCE	T_1	p_1	λ_1	h_0	C
Benzol	273	0.0322	10550	24.6	3.22
Water..............	273	0.0060	12110	9.0	3.44
Iodine.............	374	0.065	13940	13.7	4.04

During the past summer Naumann, a student in my laboratory, made a number of determinations of the vapor pressure of iodine at moderate temperatures, by measuring the quantities of iodine carried over by a current of hydrogen. His work is not yet finished, but the following values may be given:

TABLE VIII

$T-273$	ATMOSPHERES	
	p (obs.)	p (calc.)
−21.	0.000004	0.000005
19.	0.00024	0.00024
60.	0.0067	0.0050
85.	0.0267	0.0222
137.	0.263	0.263

According to the formulas and data given above, the vapor pressure must obey the equation

$$\log p = -\frac{14609}{4.571\,T} + 1.75 \log T - \frac{0.0143}{4.571} T + C.$$

The agreement between the observed and calculated values is sufficient, if we set

$$C = 3.925,$$

as has been done in calculating p in the above table; whereas we found above, in a very different manner,

$$C = 4.04.$$

Unfortunately the experimental data which would be required in order to apply equation (38) to the solid or liquid state are available for only a few substances. But the very probable assumption, that the curves shown in Fig. 8 extend without intersection to as high values of the abscissa $\left(\dfrac{\tau}{T}-1\right)$ as we may choose to take, furnishes us with a means of determining by a kind of interpolation the value of C for any substance if we know a single point in the curve of that substance. This procedure is rendered very much simpler by the very evident fact that the values of C become larger the more the curve for a given substance is inclined with respect to the axis of abscissas. Table IX shows this clearly; together with the values of C are given the values for a as found from equation (31) for the different substances, and corresponding to values of $\dfrac{\tau}{T}$ chosen between 1.25 and 1.40. It seemed most correct to limit the comparison to the initial parts of the curves where formula (31) evidently holds most accurately.

TABLE IX

	C	a		C	a
N_2....	2.37	2.4	Ether.........	3.56	3.0
O_2....	2.20	2.6	Chloroform....	4.07	2.9
NH_3..	3.28	3.0	Benzol........	3.15	2.85
SO_2..	3.42	3.0	Water.........	3.6	3.3
CS_2...	3.26	2.75	Alcohol.......	4.48	3.7

For substances for which it has apparently been possible to determine C with some degree of accuracy (the most uncertain are evidently oxygen and nitrogen), we find approximately

$$(39) \qquad C = 1.1\,a.$$

Table X contains the values of C calculated according to equation (39) for a considerable number of substances. These are the values which we shall use hereafter in the calculation of chemical equilibria.

TABLE X

H_2...........	2.2	N_2O....	3.3	Benzol.........	3.1
CH_4	2.5	H_2S....	3.0	Alcohol........	4.1
N_2...........	2.6	SO_2....	3.3	Ether..........	3.3
O_2..........	2.8	CO_2....	3.2	Acetone........	3.7
CO...........	3.6	CS_2	3.1	Propyl acetate..	3.8
Cl_2..........	3.0	NH_3 ...	3.3		
I_2............	4.0	H_2O....	3.7		
HCl..........	3.0	CCl_4 ...	3.1		
NO... (about)	3.7	$CHCl_3$..	3.2		

From these figures we may conclude that for substances which do not associate, C increases quite regularly with the boiling point, so that we can interpolate with a fair degree of certainty the values of C for other substances which are not associated; whereas associated substances (water, alcohol, acetone, probably NO, perhaps also CO) have distinctly higher values than would correspond to their boiling points.

Systematic observations, especially by the extension of the measurements of vapor pressures down to very low temperatures, and also the determination of specific heats between wide limits, would therefore probably enable us to determine with sufficient accuracy the value, for pure substances, of the integration constant, or, as it may appropriately be called, the *chemical constant C.*

LECTURE VIII

THE CALCULATION OF CHEMICAL EQUILIBRIA IN HOMOGENEOUS GASEOUS SYSTEMS

For the calculation of the equilibrium in a gaseous system we developed equations (22) and (29), which can be combined to the following:

$$ln\,K = -\frac{Q_0'}{RT} + \frac{\Sigma\nu a}{R}\,ln\,T + \frac{\Sigma\nu\beta}{R}T + \Sigma\nu i.$$

Introducing, as before, partial pressures in place of concentrations, and letting

$$K' = \frac{p_1{}^{\nu_1}\,p_2{}^{\nu_2}\cdots\cdots}{p_1{}'^{\nu_1'}\cdots\cdots},$$

we have

$$(40)\quad ln\,K' = -\frac{Q_0'}{RT} + \frac{\Sigma\nu(a+R)}{R}\,ln\,T$$

$$+ \frac{\Sigma\nu\beta}{R}T + \Sigma\nu(i+ln\,R).$$

Moreover, according to (15) and (16),

$$\Sigma\nu(a+R) = \Sigma\nu H_p{}^0 = \Sigma\nu\,3.5,$$

and by equation (36)

$$C = \frac{i+ln\,R}{2.303}.$$

Substituting these values we obtain, finally,

$$(41) \quad \log K' = -\frac{Q_0'}{4.571\,T} + \Sigma\nu\,1.75\log T$$

$$+ \frac{\Sigma\nu\beta}{4.571}\,T + \Sigma\nu\,C.$$

For the calculation of β equations (15) and (32) are employed, according to which

$$H_p = H_p^0 + 2\beta T = 3.5 + a_0 + 2\beta T,$$

where H_p denotes the molecular heat at any given temperature T, and hence

$$(42) \qquad \Sigma\nu\beta = \frac{\Sigma\nu\,H_p - \Sigma\nu\,3.5}{2\,T},$$

since by equation (24)

$$\Sigma\nu a_0 = 0.$$

Finally, it may be recalled that if we represent the heat of a reaction at constant pressure by Q_p', we have the equation

$$Q_p' = Q_0' + \Sigma\nu\,3.5\,T + \Sigma\nu\beta\,T^2.$$

As the first application of the above formulas, let us discuss the equilibrium between two optical antipodes, to which my Berlin colleague van't Hoff directed my attention in a conversation. The equation of the reaction is

$$(d)\ A_1 = (l)\ A_1',$$

and if p_1 and p_1' denote the partial pressures corresponding to this homogeneous gaseous equilibrium, our formula gives

$$ln\,K' = ln\frac{p_1}{p_1'} = -\frac{Q_0'}{RT} + \frac{\Sigma\nu(a+R)}{R}ln\,T$$
$$ + \frac{\Sigma\nu\beta T}{R} + \Sigma\nu(i + ln\,R).$$

Q_0' is here zero, as is well known, and, since the specific heats of the two forms are exactly equal to each other,

$$\Sigma\nu(a+R) = 0, \quad \Sigma\nu\beta = 0, \text{ etc.,}$$

and as the vapor pressures are also identical,

$$\Sigma\nu(i + ln\,R) = 0,$$

and hence

$$p_1 = p_1'.$$

Our theory yields therefore the well-known result that in the equilibrium mixture ("racemic mixture") the concentrations of the two antipodes are equal. This theorem has been proved by van't Hoff by a kinetic method. Our theory gives the result in a purely thermodynamic way.

To render the trial of our equations fairly conclusive they must be applied only to those equilibria which have been fully investigated and for which, besides the thermochemical data, the specific heats and values of C (chemical constants) are known. The number of these examples is not large, and I have been forced to use almost exclusively measurements made by myself and by my pupils during the last few years. These reactions are the following: [*]

1. $\qquad 2H_2 + O_2 = 2H_2O$
2. $\qquad 2CO + O_2 = 2CO_2$
3. $\qquad 2NO = N_2 + O_2$
4. $\qquad H_2 + Cl_2 = 2HCl$
5. $\qquad 4HCl + O_2 = 2H_2O + 2Cl_2$
6. $\qquad 2H_2 + S_2 = 2H_2S$

1. *Dissociation of Water Vapor.*—We may take here

$$\left. \begin{array}{ll} \text{for } H_2O, & H_p = 8.02 \\ \text{for } H_2 \text{ and } O_2, & H_p = 6.9 \end{array} \right\} \text{ at } T = 450.$$

Furthermore,

$$Q_p' = 116000 \text{ when } T = 373,$$

so that

$$Q_p' = 114600 + 3.5\,T + 0.0012\,T^2,$$

and

$$\log K' = -\frac{25050}{T} + 1.75 \log T + 0.00028\,T - 0.2$$

since $\quad (\Sigma \nu C = 4.4 + 2.8 - 7.4 = -0.2).$

[*]To simplify the general scheme of the reactions, the chemical equations are written so that, as read from left to right, the reaction is accompanied by the evolution of heat.

If x denotes the (very small) degree of dissociation at the pressure of one atmosphere

$$K' = \frac{x^3}{2}$$

and

$$3 \log x = - \frac{25050}{T} + 1.75 \log T + 0.00028\, T + 0.1.$$

In the following table, together with the values of the degree of dissociation, are given the corresponding temperatures as observed by Wartenberg and myself (loc. cit.), and as calculated from the above equation:

TABLE XI

$100\,x$	T (obs.)	T (calc.)
0.0189	1480	1455
0.199	1800	1745

2. *Dissociation of Carbonic Acid.*—We can set

for CO_2, $\qquad H_p = 10.05,$ $\Big\}$ at $T = 473.$
for CO and O_2, $H_p = 6.9,$

Also since

$$Q_p' = 136000 \text{ when } T = 290,$$
$$Q_p' = 135300 + 3.5\,T - 0.0030\,T^2,$$

and

$$\log K' = - \frac{29600}{T} + 1.75 \log T - 0.00066\,T + 3.6$$
$$(\Sigma \nu C = 7.2 + 2.8 - 6.4 = 3.6);$$

and, exactly as in the case of water vapor,

$$3\log x = -\frac{29600}{T} + 1.75\log T - 0.00066\,T + 3.9.$$

The agreement between the calculated values and those observed by Wartenberg and myself is shown in the following table:

TABLE XII

$100\,x$	T (obs.)	T (calc.)
0.00419	1300	1369
0.029	1478	1552

For the ordinary temperature ($T = 290$) the formulas give

$$\text{for } H_2O, \quad 100x = 10^{-25.31},$$
$$\text{for } CO_2, \quad 100x = 10^{-29.35};$$

whereas by calculating from the measurements of Wartenberg and myself with the aid of the second law of thermodynamics, we find

$$\text{for } H_2O, \quad 100x = 10^{-25.4},$$
$$\text{for } CO_2, \quad 100x = 10^{-29.1}.$$

The figures agree very well; probably the values calculated by the purely thermochemical method for low temperatures are even more exact than the others.

3. *Formation of Nitric Oxide.*—According to Strecker * we have here

for N_2 and O_2, $\dfrac{H_p}{H_v} = 1.40$; for NO, $\dfrac{H_p}{H_v} = 1.39$;

and since $\quad Q_p' = 43200$ when $T = 290$

$$Q_p' = 43200 + 0.0004\,T^2,$$

and $\quad \log K' = -\dfrac{9450}{T} + 0.00008\,T + 2.0$

$$(\Sigma\nu C = 7.4 - 2.6 - 2.8 = 2.0).$$

The following table (XIII) contains the values observed by me together with those calculated from the above formula. If x denotes the volume of NO formed per unit volume of atmospheric air at the temperature in question, we have

$$K' = \frac{x^2}{\left(79.2 - \dfrac{x}{2}\right)\left(20.8 - \dfrac{x}{2}\right)}.$$

TABLE XIII

x	T (obs.)	T (calc.)
0.0037	1825	1624
0.01	2205	1898

The agreement between the observed and calculated values is only approximate; but it must

* Strecker, Wiedemann's Annalen, **17**, 102.

be emphasized that the data for the curve of vapor tension of nitric oxide are very uncertain, as has also been noted by Travers,* who states that "the results obtained by Olszsewski for the vapor pressures of nitric oxide are somewhat peculiar." In fact, the curve for nitric oxide plotted according to the method used in Fig. 8 is very irregular, and only permits the conclusion that it slopes more steeply than the curves for oxygen and nitrogen, and therefore that nitric oxide must have a distinctly higher value for C than these gases. If, for example, we were to substitute for C the value 3.4 instead of 3.7 we should have in the above table 2162 instead of 1898 as the temperature corresponding to $x = 0.01$. A revision of the vapor pressure of nitric oxide seems therefore desirable, and would in itself be of interest because of the remarkable behavior of this substance.†

4. *Formation of Hydrochloric Acid.*—The specific heats of hydrogen and hydrochloric acid are practically equal to each other; the specific heat of chlorine, on the other hand, is markedly higher (Strecker). It is probable, however, that in the

---

* Travers, Experimental Study of Gases, p. 243.
† See page 76.

case of the specific heat of chlorine we are dealing with irregularities which disappear at very low pressures. Since in the following calculation (dissociation of hydrochloric acid at the ordinary temperature) only exceedingly low pressures are involved, and still more because it is in any case a question of only a very small correction, we may set

$$\Sigma \nu H_p = 0,$$

and therefore $\qquad \Sigma \nu \beta = 0.$

As the heat of formation of hydrochloric acid is 22000, we obtain

$$\log K' = \log x^2 = -\frac{44000}{4.571\,T} + 2.2 + 3.0 - 6.0$$

or

$$\log x = -\frac{4813}{T} - 0.4,$$

in which x denotes again the (very small) degree of dissociation.

Dolezalek * has measured with great care the electromotive force of the hydrogen-chlorine cell. According to the usual formulas this electromotive force can be calculated from

$$\epsilon = \frac{R\,T}{F}\,ln\,\frac{p}{\pi x},$$

* Dolezalek, Ztschr. f. phys. Chem., **26**, 334.

in which p denotes the partial pressure of the hydrogen and of the chlorine at the electrodes, and π the partial pressure of the hydrochloric acid over the solution used. In the article referred to it is shown that the electromotive force is dependent on the partial pressure of the hydrochloric acid as given in the above formula. It will suffice, therefore, to calculate one value. Choosing for this purpose an experiment in which the concentration of the hydrochloric acid was six times normal, we find in the paper of Dolezalek

$$\pi = 0.52 \text{ mm}, \quad p = 750 \text{ mm},$$

and since the temperature was 30°,

$$\epsilon = 0.0601 \left(\log \frac{750}{\pi} + \frac{4813}{T} + 0.4 \right) = 1.168 \text{ volts},$$

while Dolezalek gives the measured value **1.160** volts. The agreement is excellent, and this example shows at the same time how our theory enables us to calculate electromotive forces from thermal data. The calculation according to the Helmholtz-Thomson rule, by which the chemical energy is simply put equal to the electrical, gives in this case, as is well known, a value which is much too great (about **1.4** volts).

For the equilibria

$$2\,NO = N_2 + O_2$$

and $$H_2 + Cl_2 = 2\,HCl,$$

our theory gave

$$\log K' = -\frac{9450}{T} + 1.4,$$

and $$\log K' = -\frac{9626}{T} - 0.8,$$

respectively.

The constant of integration, I, is positive in the first case and negative in the second, which corresponds to the fact that the vapor pressure curve of NO drawn as in Fig. 8 is very much, that of H_2 very slightly, inclined with respect to the axis of abscissas. These simple examples show how different facts are correlated by our theory.

LECTURE IX

THE CALCULATION OF CHEMICAL EQUILIBRIA IN HOMOGENEOUS GASEOUS SYSTEMS.— (*Concluded*)

CONTINUING the application of our equations to the reactions mentioned in the previous lecture we may consider next

5. *The Deacon Process.*

$$4\,HCl + O_2 = 2\,H_2O + 2\,Cl_2.$$

This reaction was studied by Dr. Vogel von Falkenstein, the first account of the work being published in the *Zeitschrift für Elektrochemie.**

We found for the dissociation of water vapor

$$\log \frac{[H_2]^2\,[O_2]}{[H_2O]^2} = -\frac{25050}{T} + 1.75 \log T + 0.00028\,T + 0.1,$$

and for the dissociation of hydrochloric acid,

$$\log \frac{[H_2]\,[Cl_2]}{[HCl]^2} = -\frac{9626}{T} - 0.8.$$

By combining these two equations the above

* Vol. **12**, p. 763.

equilibrium can be calculated (as Bodländer* first pointed out) and we thus obtain

$$\log \frac{[H_2O]^2 [Cl_2]_4^2}{[O_2] [HCl]} = \log K' = \frac{5790}{T} - 1.75 \log T$$
$$- 0.00028\, T - 1.4.$$

Table XIV shows the agreement between the values of K' found in the very careful investigation of Vogel von Falkenstein and the values calculated by the theoretical formula.

TABLE XIV

$T - 273$	K' (obs.)	K' (calc.)	$\log K'$ (obs.)	$\log K'$ (calc.)
450	31.0	31.9	1.49	1.50
600	0.893	0.98	−0.050	−0.009
650	0.398	0.371	−0.400	−0.430

We see, therefore, that the equilibrium in the Deacon Process can be calculated from our theory very accurately.

The above examples show, first, that we can place

$$Q_p' = Q_0'$$

without appreciable error; and secondly, that if the temperature is not too high the term containing T as a factor may be disregarded. The numerical calculations are thereby very much simplified.

* Bodländer, Ztschr. f. phys. Chem., **27,** 55.

6. *Formation of Hydrogen Sulphide.*

$$2\,H_2 + S_2 = 2\,H_2S.$$

During the past summer Dr. Prenner has studied this reaction in my laboratory, using the method of semipermeable membranes. He obtained the following values for the partial pressure of hydrogen, when the total pressure of the hydrogen sulphide was equal to one atmosphere.

TABLE XV

T	p (cm. Hg)	K'
1100	6.5	4.1×10^{-4}
1220	11.5	2.9×10^{-3}
1320	16.2	1.05×10^{-2}
1420	20.8	2.96×10^{-2}
1520	25.4	7.5×10^{-2}

Since sulphur vapor is diatomic at these temperatures, the law of mass action gives

$$K' = \frac{[H_2]^2\,[S_2]}{[H_2S]^2}.$$

Using the second law of thermodynamics, Preuner found for the heat of reaction at constant volume 38000 gram calories. Since we do not know the specific heat of hydrogen sulphide at high temperatures, we can only use the approximate formula

$$\log K' = -\frac{38000}{4.6\,T} + 1.75 \log T + 1.3$$

$$(\Sigma \nu C = 4.4 + 2.9 - 6.0 = 1.3).$$

The theoretical formula gives for $K' = 2.9 \times 10^{-3}$ the temperature $T = 920$, instead of 1220 as observed; and for $K' = 2.96 \times 10^{-2}$ the temperature $T = 1020$, instead of 1420 as observed.

The difference between the observed and the calculated data seems to indicate that the specific heat of hydrogen sulphide increases rather rapidly at high temperatures, but it must be stated that the above value of Q may not be quite correct.

Some of the values given by other experimenters for equilibria in homogeneous gaseous systems may now be utilized for the trial of our formulas.

(7) *Formation of Sulphur Trioxide* (calculated by Dr. Falk).—The reaction is

$$2SO_2 + O_2 = 2SO_3.$$

Placing

for O_2, $H_p = 6.9$,

for SO_2, $H_p = 9.8$ (Regnault),   at $T = 430$,

for SO_3, $H_p = 11.0$,

$$\Sigma \nu \beta = \frac{1.0}{860} = 0.0011.$$

The value of H_p for SO_3 has never been determined, but it seems reasonable to place it a little higher than that of SO_2. In any case, the effect on the final calculation is small, for if we should take for SO_3, $H_p = 11.5$, instead of 11.0 as above, the calculated temperatures given in the following table (**XVI**) would each be increased by only about 25°.

Furthermore, since $Q_p' = 45200$ when $T = 290$, and therefore $Q_p' = 44100 + 3.5\,T + 0.0011\,T^2$, we have

$$\log K' = -\frac{9600}{T} + 1.75 \log T + 0.00024\,T + 3.2$$

($\Sigma\nu C = 6.6 + 2.8 - 6.2 = 3.2$, C for SO_3 being put equal to 3.1 as no experimental data for its calculation are available.)

TABLE XVI

K'	T (obs. by Bodenstein) *	T (calc.)
0.0053	852.	885.
0.29	1000.	1036.
7.81	1170.	1202.

(8) *Formation of Ammonia.*—The formation of this substance, the specific heat of which is not

* Measurements of Bodenstein quoted by Haber, "Thermodynamik technischer Gasreaktionen."

definitely known, has been studied by Haber.* The heat of formation of ammonia is about 12000 gram calories per mol, and if we consider an equivalent mixture of hydrogen and nitrogen, as Haber does, denoting by x the (small) partial pressure of the ammonia formed, we should have

$$\log K' = \log \frac{(0.75)^3 \cdot 0.25}{x^2} = -\frac{24000}{4.571\,T} + 3.5 \log T + 6.6 + 2.6 - 6.6,$$

or

$$\log \frac{0.325}{x} = -\frac{2625}{T} + 1.75 \log T + 1.3,$$

from which we find by calculation that the value $x = 1.2 \times 10^{-4}$ corresponds to an absolute temperature of 893, whereas Haber found experimentally 1293.

I was astonished at this difference, and since Haber only determined the equilibrium at one temperature, Dr. Jellinek, my assistant, and I have begun to investigate this equilibrium. The values which we have found are, in fact, rather different, and in much better agreement with the theory. This case, important in itself, will be studied very carefully.

For an approximate calculation we may em-

* Haber, "Thermodynamik technischer Gasreaktionen," p. 185.

ploy, as the foregoing results have shown, the following rules:

1. In place of Q_0' we may substitute Q_p', the heat of reaction at constant pressure at ordinary temperatures, and the term containing T as a factor may be disregarded.

2. If we have no certain data for the chemical constant C, the average value 3.0 may be used.

In this way Dr. Brill[*] has collected and calculated all the available examples of dissociation where the reaction follows an equation of the type

$$A_1 = A_1' + A_2'.$$

If x denotes the degree of dissociation and P the total pressure

$$p_1 = \frac{1-x}{1+x}P, \quad p_1' = p_2' = \frac{x}{1+x}P,$$

and therefore

$$K' = \frac{x^2}{(1-x^2)}P.$$

For $x = 0.5$ we obtain the approximate formula

$$(42a) \quad -\log 3 = -\frac{Q_p'}{4.571\,T} + 1.75 \log T + 3.0 -$$

$\log P$, in which P is expressed in atmospheres.

The following examples were found in the literature:

[*] Brill, Ztschr. f. phys. Chem., **57**, 721.

Table XVII

Dissociation of	P (atm.)	$Q_p{}'$	T (obs.)	T (calc.)
N_2O_4	0.655	13000.	323.1	348.0
Formic acid	1.00	15000.	410.0	410.0
Acetic acid	1.00	17000.	430.0	455.0
Bromamylenhydrate	1.00	19500.	483.0	515.0
"	0.10	19500.	462.0	468.0
Bromine $(x = 0.1)$	0.078	59800.	1270.	1250.

It may be added that measurements of the dissociation of iodine vapor also exist, but as they were made by the Victor Meyer method in which the partial pressures are not definite, the values are not accurate enough for the evaluation of Q.

Table XVIII gives the values of $Q_p{}'$ and T, derived from equation (42a), which correspond to a dissociation of $x = 0.5$, and a pressure of one atmosphere.

Table XVIII

$Q_p{}'$	T
10000	290
15000	405
20000	525
30000	780
50000	1220
100000	2350
200000	4500

LECTURE X

THE CALCULATION OF CHEMICAL EQUILIBRIA IN HETEROGENEOUS SYSTEMS AND OF ELECTROMOTIVE FORCES

IT can easily be shown that the treatment of heterogeneous systems can be reduced to the consideration of a homogeneous system together with the various equilibria of vaporization or of sublimation. Let us consider a reaction of the type

$$na + \nu_1 A_1 + \nu_2 A_2 + \cdots = \nu_1' A_1' + \cdots,$$

in which a denotes a species of molecule coexisting in the pure state (solid or liquid) with the gaseous phase. For the gaseous phase the following equation holds:

$$ln\, K' + \frac{Q_0'}{RT} - \frac{\Sigma \nu (a + R)}{R} ln\, T - \frac{\Sigma \nu \beta}{R} T$$
$$- (n + \Sigma \nu)(i + ln\, R) = 0.$$

On the other hand, equation (30) multiplied by n gives for the coexistence of a saturated vapor with its solid or liquid form

$$ln\,p^n + \frac{n\lambda_0}{RT} - \frac{n(a - a_0 + R)}{R}\,ln\,T$$

$$- \frac{n(\beta - \beta_0)}{R}\,T - n(i + ln\,R) = 0.$$

Subtracting the latter equation from the former, all the expressions in the first, third, and fifth terms relating to the solid or liquid drop out, $a + R$ and $a - a_0 + R$ being both equal to 3.5. The second term becomes, as before, the heat of reaction divided by T, and for the calculation of the term which is multiplied by T we have finally the expression, similar to equation (42),

$$\frac{h + \Sigma\nu H_p - \Sigma\nu\,3.5}{2\,T},$$

in which h denotes the molecular heat of the species of molecule a in the condensed state at the temperature T.

The same equations evidently hold when any number of solid or liquid bodies coexist, provided that all are in the pure state. We then have the general expression, analogous to equation (41)

$$(43) \quad \log K = - \frac{Q_0}{4.571\,T} + \Sigma\nu\,1.75\log T$$

$$+ \frac{\Sigma n\beta_0 + \Sigma\nu\beta}{4.571}\,T + \Sigma\nu C,$$

in which Q_0 denotes the heat developed by the reaction, and also

$$(44) \quad \Sigma(n\beta_0 + \nu\beta) = \frac{\Sigma nh + \Sigma\nu H_p - \Sigma\nu\, 3.5}{2\,T}.$$

In calculating the remaining terms the species of molecules A, present only in the gaseous state, must be taken into account. Examples to which equation (43) can be applied are very numerous; the calculation of β, however, on account of the lack of exact data concerning the specific heats, is possible in only a few cases.

1. *Formation of Hydrocyanic Acid.*—Dr. Wartenberg studied last summer the equilibrium

$$2C + N_2 + H_2 = 2HCN.$$

If equal volumes of nitrogen and hydrogen are taken, and x denotes the fraction by volume of the original mixture transformed into hydrocyanic acid, we have

$$p_1 = \left(0.5 - \frac{x}{2}\right) \text{ atmosphere};$$

$$p_2 = \left(0.5 - \frac{x}{2}\right) \text{ atmosphere};$$

$$p_1' = x \text{ atmosphere};$$

and therefore

$$\log K = \log \frac{\left(0.5 - \dfrac{x}{2}\right)^2}{x^2} = \frac{13060}{T} + 2.6 + 2.2 - 2C',$$

where C' is the chemical constant for hydrocyanic

acid. The following table contains the results obtained by Wartenberg:

TABLE XIX

$100\,x$	T (obs.)	T (calc.)$_\mathrm{I}$	T (calc.)$_\mathrm{II}$
1.95	1908	2174	1908
3.1	2025	2336	2032
4.7	2148	2503	2155

The values T (calc.)$_\mathrm{I}$ were obtained by putting C' (for HCN) $= 4.0$, T (calc.)$_\mathrm{II}$ by putting $C' = 4.425$.

A large value for the chemical constant of hydrocyanic acid would be expected from its high dielectric constant (90) and its great dissociating power, and it is therefore probable that the value in question is greater than that for water (3.7).

2. *Formation of Carbon Bisulphide.*—The equilibrium

$$C + S_2 = CS_2$$

was measured by Koref. The heat of reaction at high temperatures can be calculated from the heat of reaction at ordinary temperatures and the difference in energy between solid sulphur and sulphur vapor S_2. The latter is obtainable from the experiments of Preuner on the heat of formation of hydrogen sulphide at high temperatures, by comparison with its heat of formation at ordinary temperatures.　Placing $\Sigma \nu C = 2.9 - 3.1 = - 0.2$, we find

$$\log \frac{[S_2]}{[CS_2]} = - \frac{8000}{4.571\, T} - 0.2.$$

The following table contains the percentages by volume of CS_2 formed at different temperatures, together with the temperatures calculated from our theory:

TABLE XX

$100\,x$	T (obs.)	T (calc.)
1.15	900.	1000.
1.9	1000.	1150.
3.2	1100.	1300.

In this case the agreement between the observed and calculated temperatures would be better if $\Sigma \nu C$ were set equal to zero instead of $- 0.2$.

3. *Dissociation of Ammonium Hydrosulphide.* —Calculating the molecular heat of this substance according to Kopp's method as 19.1 when $T = 300$, and taking for the molecular heat of ammonia 9.5, and for that of hydrogen sulphide 8.5, we obtain, since the heat of dissociation at constant pressure is 22800 at ordinary temperatures,

$$Q' = 21900 + 7.0\, T - 0.013\, T^2.$$

Denoting the dissociation pressure by P, we have

$$\tfrac{1}{2} \log K = \log \frac{P}{2} = -\frac{2396}{T} + 1.75 \log T$$
$$- 0.0014\,T + 3.15.$$

For $T = 298.1$, the dissociation pressure is 0.661 atmosphere; from the above equation the corresponding temperature is calculated to be 318.

With the approximate formula

$$\log \frac{P}{2} = -\frac{11400}{4.571\,T} + 1.75 \log T + 3.15$$

the calculation gives a temperature of 312. Since the determination of the coefficient of T, as remarked several times, is rather uncertain, and since the approximate formula obtained from equation (43) by putting

$$Q_0 = Q', \text{ and } \Sigma(n\beta_0 + \nu\beta) = 0,$$

gives only slightly different values, we shall in general use this approximate formula in the following examples.

4. *Vapor Tension of Sodium Phosphate.*— Frowein * found the vapor tension of the salt $Na_2HPO_4 \cdot 12H_2O$, for $T = 283.8$, to be 0.00842 atmosphere; the heat of hydration, in agreement with the calorimetric value, is calculated from the change in vapor tension with the tempera-

* Frowein, Ztschr. f. phys. Chem., **1**, 362.

ture to be 2244; and the heat of dissociation is $2244 + 10586 = 12830$. We have, therefore,

$$\log p = -\frac{12830}{4.57\,T} + 1.75 \log T + 3.7,$$

from which we find by calculation a temperature of 279 (instead of 284) for the above pressure. Since there are many exact measurements at hand concerning the dissociation of salts containing water of crystallization, the study of the specific heats of the salts in question for the purpose of testing the more exact formula (43) would appear desirable.

5. *Revision of Trouton's Rule.*—The empirical relation known as "Trouton's Rule," which is formulated

$$\frac{\lambda}{T_0} = \text{constant},$$

where λ is the molecular heat of vaporization, and T_3 the boiling point of the substance on the absolute scale of temperature, has been supposed up to the present time to be at least approximately correct.

A closer examination taking into account substances having widely different boiling temperatures shows, however, as I wish to demonstrate at this point, that the above quotient is not by any means constant, but increases regularly with the boiling temperature.

In the thermodynamic calculation of heats of vaporization, account must be taken of the fact that at the boiling point, especially of substances whose molecules are large, the saturated vapors no longer strictly obey the gas laws. From the formulas (34) and (35) we can obtain

$$\lambda = R\,\frac{T_1 T_2}{T_1 - T_2}\left(1 - \frac{p}{\pi}\right)ln\,\frac{p_1}{p_2},$$

in which p_1 and p_2 denote the vapor pressures corresponding to T_1 and T_2, two temperatures which differ by so small an amount that their geometrical and arithmetical means may for practical purposes be set equal to one another. This mean temperature is the one to which λ corresponds.

This formula gives in fact values which agree with the direct measurements; in general the heats of vaporization calculated with its aid are more accurate than those determined calorimetrically.

In Table XXI are given the values for the boiling point T_0, and the heat of vaporization λ at this temperature, calculated from the above formula; for hydrogen alone the calorimetrically determined and very accurate value given by Dewar, has been introduced.

TABLE XXI

Substance	T_0	λ	$\dfrac{\lambda}{T_0}$	$9.5 \log T$ $-0.007\, T_0$
Hydrogen............	20.4	248	12.2	12.3
Nitrogen............	77.5	1362	17.6	17.4
Argon...............	86.0	1460	17.0	17.8
Oxygen.............	90.6	1664	18.3	18.0
Methane............	108.	1951	18.0	18.6
Ethyl ether.........	307.	6466	21.1	21.5
Carbon bisulphide...	319.	6490	20.4	21.6
Benzol..............	353.	7497	21.2	21.7
Propyl acetate.......	375.	8310	22.2	21.8
Aniline.............	457.	10500	23.0	22.1
Methyl salicylate.....	497.	11000	22.2	22.1

It is evident that $\dfrac{\lambda}{T_0}$ increases decidedly and regularly with the boiling temperature. The expression given in the last column,

$$\frac{\lambda}{T_0} = 9.5 \log T_0 - 0.007\, T_0$$

(which I have derived from certain considerations which I shall not give in detail here) agrees very well with the observations, and may perhaps be called the "Revised Rule of Trouton."

Substances which are polymerized in the liquid state, but have the normal vapor densities in the form of gas, have higher values for the quotient $\dfrac{\lambda}{T_0}$ than are calculated from the above formula.

A rule very similar to the rule of Trouton has been proposed by Le Chatelier and further discussed by Forcrand.* According to this relation

$$\frac{Q'}{T} = \text{constant},$$

in which Q' denotes the heat developed in the dissociation of one mol of the substance and T the temperature at which the dissociation pressure is equal to one atmosphere. The value of the constant is found to be about 33.

As an example of this rule, we shall consider

6. *The Dissociation of Metal-Ammonia Chlorides.*—Forcrand gives a *résumé* of the heats of dissociation, determined for constant pressure at the ordinary temperature, and the absolute temperatures at which the vapor tensions become equal to the atmospheric pressure. Every third value has been taken from the table of Forcrand.

* Forcrand, Ann. de chim. et de phys., [7] **28**, 545.

TABLE XXII

	Q' (calories)	T	$\dfrac{Q'}{T}$
$ZnCl_2 + 6NH_3$	11000	332	33.13
$CaCl_2 + 4NH_3$	10290	315	32.66
$2AgCl + 3NH_3$	11580	341	33.96
$PdCl_2 + 4NH_3$	15560	483	32.22
$LiCl + 2NH_3$	11600	367	31.61
$CuCl_2 + 6NH_3$	11150	363	30.72

The expression $\dfrac{Q'}{T}$ is fairly constant, and Forcrand finds this confirmed by all the ammonia compounds investigated. This regularity is not only suggestive of Trouton's Rule, but from the following considerations the constancy appears here also to be limited to a certain range of temperature.

To apply equation (43) we may set, according to Kopp, the molecular heat of solid ammonium chloride equal to 20.0; for solid hydrochloric acid the value 8.6 may be calculated, so that for solid ammonia 11.4 remains. Substituting for the molecular heat of gaseous ammonia 9.5, we have, from equation (44)

$$Q' = Q_0 + 3.5\,T - 0.009\,T^2,$$

and further

$$\log p = -\frac{Q_0}{4.571\,T} - 1.75 \log T - 0.002\,T + 3.3,$$

from which, putting $p = 1$, we obtain for the coefficient $\dfrac{Q'}{T}$

$$\frac{Q'}{T} = 3.5\,\frac{290}{T} - 0.009\,\frac{(290)^2}{T}$$
$$+ (1.75\log T - 0.002\,T + 3.3)\,4.571.$$

The second member reduces for $T = 290$, to the value 33.2; for $T = 358$, to 32.9. We see, then, that as given by this equation, $\dfrac{Q'}{T}$ must necessarily be constant over a rather wide range of temperature in agreement with the empirical rule of Le Chatelier-Forcrand; and that the value which we have calculated theoretically does in fact agree completely with the average value obtained from Forcrand's data, that is, 32.33 at an average temperature of 358.

In general, our theory furnishes as an approximate formula for the dissociation pressure p (denoting as above by Q' the heat of dissociation per mol at constant pressure and the ordinary temperature) the following:

$$(45) \quad \log p = - \frac{Q'}{4.571\,T} + 1.75\log T + C.$$

Since the values of C lie in the vicinity of 3.0, we

obtain, independently of the nature of the substance in question, the values

$$\frac{Q'}{T} = 29.7 \quad \text{when } T = \ 100,$$
$$\text{``} \ = 33.6 \quad \text{``} \quad T = \ 300,$$
$$\text{``} \ = 35.3 \quad \text{``} \quad T = \ 500,$$
$$\text{``} \ = 37.7 \quad \text{``} \quad T = 1000.$$

In this we easily recognize the rule of Le Chatelier-Forcrand (according to which the value of $\frac{Q'}{T}$ is about 33 for widely different gases), but with this difference, that the hitherto entirely empirical coefficient 33 has acquired a simple meaning, $4.57 \ (1.75 \log T + C)$, and that the reliability of the rule is obviously limited to a middle, though rather extended, range of temperature.

In fact, if we calculate the temperature at which the dissociation pressure is equal to one atmosphere, for cases in which that temperature is very high, we find the rule of Le Chatelier-Forcrand does not hold, but that our theory gives a satisfactory agreement, as is shown by the following table collected by Dr. Brill:

TABLE XXIII

Substance	Q'	T (obs.)	$T=\dfrac{Q'}{33.}$	$T\left(\substack{\text{from}\\\text{eq. (45)}}\right)$	Observer
Ag_2CO_3 ..	20060	498	608	498	.. Joulin
$PbCO_3$ ...	22580	575	684	575	.. Colson
$CaCO_3$ ...	42520	1098	1290	1098	.... Brill
$SrCO_3$....	55770	1428	1688	1428	.... Brill

It seems very remarkable that these values which are obtained from equation (45) by putting $p = 1$, and $C = 3.2$ for CO_2 should agree entirely with the observed values; while those in the fourth column calculated according to the rule of Le Chatelier-Forcrand show a poor agreement.

Moreover, if we consider the evolution of CO in the well-known reaction of the formation of calcium carbide

$$CaC_2 + CO = CaO + 3C + 94750 \text{ cal.},$$

we find for the quotient $\dfrac{Q'}{T}$, according to the investigation of Rothmund,* $\dfrac{94570}{2040} = 46.8$, that is, a much higher value than 33, the one given by the above rule, but in better accordance with the approximate value $4.57(1.75 \log 2040 + 3.6) = 42.9$.

* Rothmund, Göttinger Nachrichten, 1901, Heft 3.

Determination of the Stability of Chemical Compounds

The question whether a chemical compound can be formed to an appreciable extent under given conditions, is identical with the question of its stability. This question can be answered by the formulas developed here with the aid of the heats of reaction. Since in general, under given experimental conditions, chemical compounds are either very stable or very unstable, owing to the fact that, especially at low temperatures, chemical equilibria in which all the components coexist in appreciable concentrations are the exception rather than the rule, our formula even in the approximate form will generally give a sufficiently definite answer.

We have already seen that ammonia, for instance, which doubles in volume when it dissociates at constant pressure, is unstable at moderately high temperatures notwithstanding that its heat of formation is by no means small. Ozone must be unstable at low temperatures, and only able to coexist to an appreciable extent with ordinary oxygen at very high temperatures, because its heat of formation is negative, and it dissociates with increase in volume. The halogen hydrides dissociate without change of volume; here a considerable heat of formation corresponds, at least at low temperatures, to great stability (*HCl, HBr*); hydriodic acid, on the other hand, which is formed from its components in the gaseous state without any marked thermal effect, exists at low temperatures in a state of equilibrium with appreciable quantities of its products of dissociation. Evidently the task of working over the whole field of chemistry from the point of view of thermochemistry lies before us. In the field of carbon compounds in particular, where the question of stability has remained almost wholly unanswered up to the present time, much light is to be expected. Thanks to the determinations of the heats of combustion, the thermochemistry of organic compounds is very accurately known, and a thorough investigation of the question of stability is thus made possible.

To mention only a few examples, let us recall first that the formation of gaseous ethyl acetate and water from alcohol vapor and acetic acid vapor takes place without the development of an appreciable amount of heat. Since the reaction goes on without change of volume, an equilibrium must be reached at which all the components are present in appreciable concentrations. Moreover, since the vapor pressures of the four substances do not differ very much from each other, this equilibrium must also exist in the liquid mixture. This will be recognized as the classic example of a chemical equilibrium, studied by Berthelot.

For the formation of acetylene from carbon and hydrogen we have the equation

$$(a) \qquad \log \frac{[H_2]}{[C_2H_2]} = \frac{11610}{T} - 0.8,$$

and for benzol the corresponding equation

$$(b) \qquad \log \frac{[H_2]^3}{[C_6H_6]} = \frac{3740}{T} + 3.5 \log T + 3.5.$$

Only at very high temperatures would the right side of equation (a) have the value, for example, of 3.0, that is, only then would 0.1 per cent by volume of acetylene be stable in the presence of hydrogen at atmospheric pressure. This corresponds evidently to the well-known formation of acetylene when an electric arc is formed between carbon electrodes in an atmosphere of hydrogen. Benzol vapor, on the other hand, in the presence of hydrogen and solid carbon, has no evident "right to exist" in appreciable amounts.

Multiplying equation (*a*) by 3 and subtracting (*b*) we have

$$\log \frac{[C_6H_6]}{[C_2H_2]^3} = \frac{31100}{T} - 3.5 \log T - 5.9.$$

This equation shows, in agreement with experiment, that acetylene, except at extremely high temperatures, may polymerize with the formation of benzol.

It would appear then that the exceptionally rich field of the equilibrium between carbon, hydrogen, and the various hydrocarbons, would furnish ample opportunity for the application of our theory.

CALCULATION OF ELECTROMOTIVE FORCES

It is evident that the calculation of the change in free energy by means of thermal data also enables us to calculate electromotive forces, as was shown in the eighth lecture. We shall now consider a few additional examples:

1. *The Oxygen-Hydrogen Cell.*—The second law of thermodynamics gives us the relation

$$(46) \qquad \epsilon = \frac{RT}{4} \ln \frac{1}{\pi_1^2 \pi_2},$$

in which π_1 and π_2 denote the partial pressures of hydrogen and oxygen in saturated water vapor. Using the formula developed in the fourth lecture, we find for the dissociation of water vapor referred to atmospheric pressure at $T = 290°$ ($t = 17°$ C), $x = 0.48 \times 10^{-25}$ per cent. Reduced to the tension of water vapor for this temperature,

$$x = \frac{0.48 \times 10^{-25}}{\sqrt[3]{0.0191}} = 1.80 \times 10^{-25} \text{ per cent,}$$

from which

$$\pi_1 = 0.0191 \times 1.80 \times 10^{-27} \text{ atmospheres,} \quad \text{and}$$

$$\pi_2 = \frac{0.0191 \times 1.80 \times 10^{-27}}{2} \text{ atmospheres.}$$

We find, therefore,

$$\epsilon = 0.01438 \log 4.92 \times 10^{85}$$
$$= 1.2322 \text{ volts at } 17° \text{ C.}$$

This value is somewhat higher than the one found by direct measurement (1.15 volts), but it seems certain that the experimental result is too low, owing to the fact that the oxygen electrode never becomes completely saturated with oxygen.*

Without using the values found by the direct experimental determination of the dissociation of water vapor, we calculated in the eighth lecture from thermochemical data the value

$$x = 10^{-25\,31}.$$

* Nernst und Wartenberg, Ztschr. f. phys. Chem., **56**, 544.

Introducing this in equation (46), we find

$$\epsilon = 1.231 \text{ volts,}$$

in excellent agreement with the value found above.

A more direct method is based upon equation (43). For the example in question this formula becomes

$$\log K = \log \pi^2 \pi_2 = -\frac{Q_0}{4.571\,T} + \Sigma\nu\,1.75 \log T$$
$$+ \frac{\Sigma n\beta_0 + \Sigma\nu\beta}{4.571}\,T + \Sigma\nu C.$$

Expressing Q, the heat of formation at constant pressure of two molecules of liquid water, by the relation

$$Q = 137400 + 10.5\,T - 0.044\,T^2,$$

which fulfills the conditions

$$Q = 2 \times 68400 \text{ when } T = 290,$$
$$\frac{dQ}{dT} = 3 \times 3.5 \text{ when } T = 0, \text{ and}$$
$$\frac{dQ}{dT} = -15.6 = 3 \times 6.8 - 36 \text{ when } T = 290.$$

We have, therefore,

$$\log \pi_1^2 \pi_2 = -\frac{30050}{T} + 5.25 \log T - 0.010\,T + 7.2$$
$$(\Sigma\nu C = 2 \times 2.2 + 2.8 = 7.2),$$

and consequently

$\epsilon = 0.01438 \times 86.39 = 1.242$ volts at 17° C.

The difference between this value and the one found above (1.231 volts) is accounted for by the fact that the assumption upon which this last method of calculation is based, namely, that the molecular heat of liquid water increases linearly with the temperature, is evidently not accurate. There is, however, a very simple expedient by means of which we can avoid this difficulty. If we calculate the electromotive force of the oxygen. hydrogen cell for $T = 273$, the temperature at which ice and liquid water coexist, the affinity of the reaction

$$2H_2 + O_2 = 2H_2O \text{ (ice)}$$

will, at this temperature, be identical with the electromotive force. For this reaction

$$Q = 138130 + 10.5T - 0.015T^2,$$

this equation fulfilling the condition

$$Q = 137000 + 36 \times 80 = 139880, \text{ for } T = 273.$$

We find further

$$\frac{dQ}{dT} = 3 \times 3.5 \text{ for } T = 0,$$

$$\frac{dQ}{dT} = 3 \times 6.7 - 18 = 2.1 \text{ for } T = 273$$

(18.0 = the heat capacity of two mols of ice), and finally

$$\log \pi_1^2 \pi_2 = -\frac{138130}{4.571\,T} + 5.25 \log T - 0.0032\,T + 7.2.$$

This equation gives for $T = 273$

$$\log \pi_1^2 \pi_2 = -91.56,$$

and therefore

$$\epsilon = \frac{0.05414}{4} \times 91.56 = 1.2393.$$

To find the value of this expression for $T = 290$, we apply the well-known equation

$$\epsilon - \frac{Q}{23046} = T \frac{d\epsilon}{dT}$$

to the liquid water cell, from which we find for ordinary temperatures

$$\frac{d\epsilon}{dT} = -0.00085.$$

Using this value we obtain

$$E = 1.225 \text{ volts at } T = 290.$$

This value agrees better with the first and second values calculated than with the third.

2. *The Clark Element.*—The reaction producing the current in the Clark element is represented by the equation

$$Zn + Hg_2SO_4 + 7H_2O = ZnSO_4 \cdot 7H_2O + 2Hg.$$

Our fundamental theorem is not directly applicable to this reaction, because, as Cohen * first clearly showed, the zinc sulphate formed passes into solution, combines with the water, and then as a result of the supersaturation so produced crystallizes out, carrying down further quantities of salt with it. If, however, ice is one of the solid substances present in the cell, that is to say, if we study the Clark element at the cryohydric point, the reaction takes place between pure substances, to which equations (23) and (24) are directly applicable.

Since the electromotive force at the cryohydric point of zinc sulphate ($-7°$ C.) is **1.4624** volts, we have

$$A = 2 \times 23046 \times 1.4624 = 67405, \text{ for } T = 266.$$

The evolution of heat at 17° C., the temperature to which the thermal data refer, is then

$$Q = 66600 \text{ (for } T = 290),$$

in which the value 88.7 is assumed for the latent heat of fusion of ice at this temperature, this value being derived from the latent heat of fusion at 0° C. and the difference between the specific heats of ice and water. Under these conditions, therefore, A and Q only differ by a small amount, as would follow also from equations (6) and (7),

* Cf. W. Jaeger, Normalelemente, Halle, 1902.

in view of the well-known fact that the molecular heats of solid substances are approximately additive. For the ordinary Clark element, in which the behavior of the solution also comes into consideration, there is certainly quite a large difference between the electrical and heat energies. For example, for $T = 291$, $A = 65875$ and $Q = 81130$.

Our new hypothesis, therefore, allows us to calculate the electromotive forces of galvanic elements in the following general way: The galvanic combination in question is assumed to be varied, using ice, if necessary, as one of the solid substances present, so that only perfectly pure substances (as distinct from mixtures or solutions) enter into the equation representing the reaction which produces the current. Knowing the heat evolved and the specific heats, the coefficients of equation (23) can be calculated, and consequently A and Q also. By applying the well-known laws which govern the change in electromotive force with the concentration in dilute solutions (the so-called osmotic theory of current production) the electromotive force for any concentration can be calculated.

In the equation

$$A = n \cdot E \cdot 23046 = Q_0 - T^2 \Sigma n \beta_0,$$

the coefficient $\Sigma n \beta_0$ appears in general to be small. Its influence is therefore often negligible at ordinary temperatures, especially when the electromotive forces dealt with are not too small.

CONSIDERATION OF THE KINETIC BASIS OF THE NEW THEOREM

The behavior of substances in the ideal gaseous state is, as is well known, of a very simple nature, which has found in the kinetic theory a theoretical explanation. The heat theorem considered in these lectures makes it appear probable that also in the liquid and solid states at very low temperatures matter obeys strikingly simple laws, and it may be hoped that in this way new points of view have been furnished for the development of the molecular theory.

If we now wish, in concluding our discussion, to take up briefly the question of the interpretation, from the standpoint of the molecular theory, of the two equations

$$
\left.
\begin{array}{l}
(a)\ \lim. \dfrac{dQ}{dT} = 0, \\[2em]
(b)\ \lim. \dfrac{dA}{dT} = 0,
\end{array}
\right\} \text{ when } T = 0,
$$

it is obvious that the first equation merely requires that in the neighborhood of the absolute zero, the molecular heat of a compound shall be equal to the sum of the atomic heats of the atoms composing the compound. That is, every atom of a particular element requires the same amount of heat to produce the same rise in temperature, independently of the state of aggregation, crystallized or amorphous, of the substance, and also of the nature of the other elements with which the atom of the element in question may be combined.

The interpretation of the equation

$$\lim.\frac{dA}{dT} = 0 \text{ when } T = 0$$

from the kinetic standpoint is more difficult. Since at the absolute zero the kinetic energy is zero, the maximum work is evidently given by the sum of the differences of the potential energies which the reacting atoms possess before and after the reaction. By the motion of the atoms, which corresponds to a definite elevation of the temperature above absolute zero, these potential energies are evidently changed. The above equation requires that this change shall be either infinitely small, or independent of the state in which the atom exists.

These considerations render it very probable that, as with the specific heats, the expansion by heat in the vicinity of absolute zero follows very simple laws. This indeed seems to be the case, as shown by the empirical relation discovered by Tammann,*

$$T_0 = \frac{\Delta v}{\gamma_0 - \gamma_0'}$$

(Δv denoting the change in volume at the melting point T_0, γ_0 and γ_0', the coefficients of expansion at T_0 of the two coexisting phases). This equation is in complete analogy with the relation

$$(28) \qquad T_0 = \frac{\sigma}{H_0 - H_0'}$$

(which we have found to be a consequence of equations (a) and (b)), and it appears not to be improbable that, corresponding to the relations represented by equations (a) and (b), the relation

$$(c) \qquad \frac{d\Delta v}{dT} = 0 \text{ when } T = 0$$

also holds; that is, the expansion by heat of amorphous or crystallized substances in the neighborhood of the absolute zero is a purely additive property.

* Krystallisieren und Schmelzen, p. 42.

These observations may suffice to show that the further application of the kinetic theory to the behavior of solid and liquid substances at temperatures close to the absolute zero promises to yield fresh sources of information.